# IMMERSION
*Bible Studies*

# GALATIANS, EPHESIANS, PHILIPPIANS

## Praise for IMMERSION

"IMMERSION BIBLE STUDIES is a powerful tool in helping readers to hear God speak through Scripture and to experience a deeper faith as a result."

Adam Hamilton, author of *24 Hours That Changed the World*

"This unique Bible study makes Scripture come alive for students. Through the study, students are invited to move beyond the head into the heart of faith."

Bishop Joseph W. Walker, author of *Love and Intimacy*

"If you're looking for a deeper knowledge and understanding of God's Word, you must dive into IMMERSION BIBLE STUDIES. Whether in a group setting or as an individual, you will experience God and his unconditional love for each of us in a whole new way."

Pete Wilson, founding and senior pastor of Cross Point Church

"This beautiful series helps readers become fluent in the words and thoughts of God, for purposes of illumination, strength building, and developing a closer walk with the One who loves us so."

Laurie Beth Jones, author of *Jesus, CEO* and *The Path*

"I highly commend to you IMMERSION BIBLE STUDIES, which tells us what the Bible teaches and how to apply it personally."

John Ed Mathison, author of *Treasures of the Transformed Life*

"The IMMERSION BIBLE STUDIES series is no less than a game changer. It ignites the purpose and power of Scripture by showing us how to do more than just know God or love God; it gives us the tools to love like God as well."

Shane Stanford, author of *You Can't Do Everything . . . So Do Something*

# IMMERSION
*Bible Studies*

# GALATIANS, EPHESIANS, PHILIPPIANS

Frank Ramirez

Abingdon Press

Nashville

# GALATIANS, EPHESIANS, PHILIPPIANS
## IMMERSION BIBLE STUDIES
by Frank Ramirez



**Library of Congress Cataloging-in-Publication Data**

Ramirez, Frank, 1954-
Galatians, Ephesians, Philippians / Frank Ramirez.
p. cm. -- (Immersion Bible studies)
ISBN 978-1-4267-1084-1 (curriculum—printed text: alk. paper) 1. Bible. N.T. Galatians—Textbooks. 2. Bible. N.T. Ephesians—Textbooks. 3. Bible. N.T. Philippians—Textbooks. I. Title.
BS2685.55.R36 2011
227'.06—dc22

2011000230

**Editor: Stan Purdum**
**Leader Guide Writer: Stan Purdum**

11 12 13 14 15 16 17 18 19 20—10 9 8 7 6 5 4 3 2 1

Manufactured in the United States of America

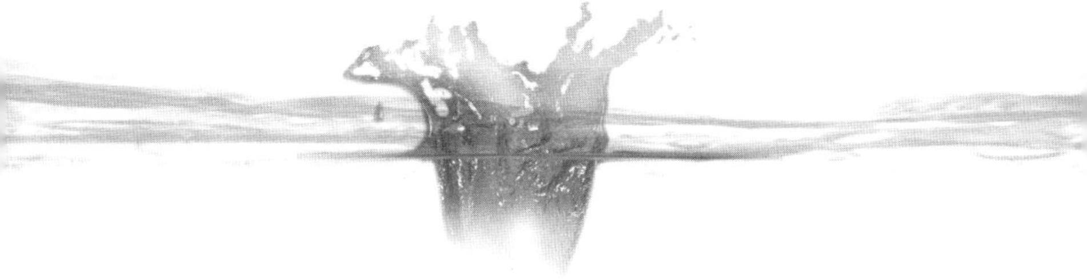

# Contents

# Review Team

Diane Blum
Pastor
East End United Methodist Church
Nashville, Tennessee

Susan Cox
Pastor
McMurry United Methodist Church
Claycomo, Missouri

Margaret Ann Crain
Professor of Christian Education
Garrett-Evangelical Theological Seminary
Evanston, Illinois

Nan Duerling
Curriculum Writer and Editor
Cambridge, Maryland

Paul Escamilla
Pastor and Writer
St. John's United Methodist Church
Austin, Texas

James Hawkins
Pastor and Writer
Smyrna, Delaware

Andrew Johnson
Professor of New Testament
Nazarene Theological Seminary
Kansas City, Missouri

Snehlata Patel
Pastor
Woodrow United Methodist Church
Staten Island, New York

Emerson B. Powery
Professor of New Testament
Messiah College
Grantham, Pennsylvania

Clayton Smith
Pastoral Staff
Church of the Resurrection
Leawood, Kansas

Harold Washington
Professor of Hebrew Bible
Saint Paul School of Theology
Kansas City, Missouri

Carol Wehrheim
Curriculum Writer and Editor
Princeton, New Jersey

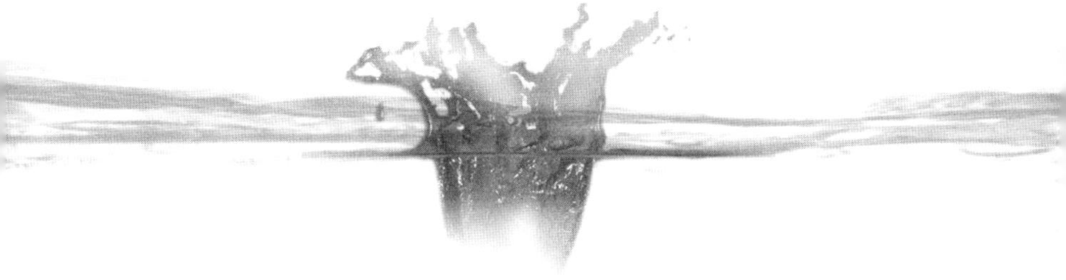

# IMMERSION BIBLE STUDIES

*A fresh new look at the Bible, from beginning to end,*
*and what it means in your life.*

Welcome to IMMERSION!

We've asked some of the leading Bible scholars, teachers, and pastors to help us with a new kind of Bible study. IMMERSION remains true to Scripture but always asks, "Where are you in your life? What do you struggle with? What makes you rejoice?" Then it helps you read the Scriptures to discover their deep, abiding truths. IMMERSION is about God and God's Word, and it is also about you—not just your thoughts, but your feelings and your faith.

In each study you will prayerfully read the Scripture and reflect on it. Then you will engage it in three ways:

*Claim Your Story*
Through stories and questions, think about your life, with its struggles and joys.

*Enter the Bible Story*
Explore Scripture and consider what God is saying to you.

*Live the Story*
Reflect on what you have discovered, and put it into practice in your life.

IMMERSION makes use of an exciting new translation of Scripture, the Common English Bible (CEB). The CEB and IMMERSION BIBLE STUDIES will offer adults:

- the emotional expectation to find the love of God
- the rational expectation to find the knowledge of God
- reliable, genuine, and credible power to transform lives
- clarity of language

Whether you are using the Common English Bible or another translation, IMMERSION BIBLE STUDIES will offer a refreshing plunge into God's Word, your life, and your life with God.

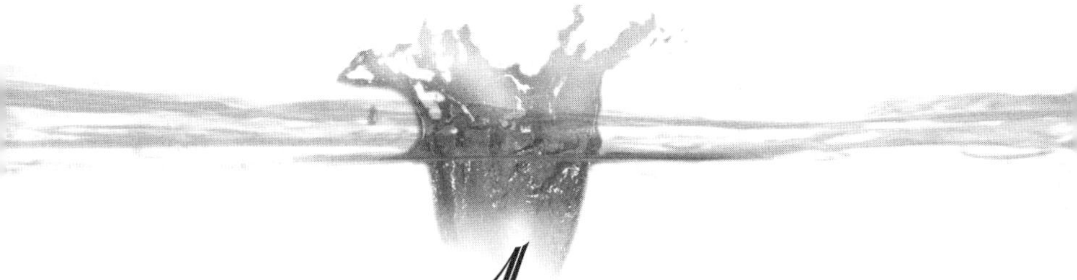

# 1.

# We Are What We Are

*Galatians 1:1–5:12*

## Claim Your Story

When I was a kid in Los Angeles, I thought everyone was just like us. I thought everyone ate *menudo* (tripe soup with hominy) and *pan dulce* (Mexican pastries) every Sunday after church. And wasn't everyone's church a huge, cavernous, cathedral-like structure? Didn't the ladies of every church's Guadalupe Society sell tamales after worship?

Now I belong to a different communion in a small town where mostly white folks eat chicken and waffles together. It's still fun—and both ways of living are compatible with serving Jesus.

We're one in Christ and different in everything else. In Galatians the apostle Paul pleads with a distinct ethnic group (you may be surprised which one) to maintain their distinctiveness and not give in to those who were trying to instill uniform cultural practices throughout Christendom.

What assumptions do you make about what is "normal"?

When it comes to our Christian faith, what is essential?

Write down a few sentences about your background, the cultures you have known, the variety of worship you've experienced, and how all this is a part of your Christian confession.

## Enter the Bible Story

### *Beginnings*

It's one of the most famous verses of Scripture in the New Testament: "There is neither Jew nor Greek; there is neither slave nor free; nor is there male and female, for you are all one in Christ Jesus" (Galatians 3:28). This gets preached, but is this true in practice? How about back then? Did the apostle Paul really expect these Galatians, whoever they were, to live this way?

Maybe we've jumped to the middle of the story and skipped the start. Let's go back to the beginning.

Here's the deal: Where we come from matters, but the one essential thing is that faith in Jesus Christ makes us family with God. Period.

This wasn't true in the Roman Empire in general. Women didn't eat with men, rich didn't eat with poor, Jew didn't eat with Greek, and slave didn't eat with free—and vice versa.

So just who were these Galatians anyway? Politically, Galatia was created by the Romans, who cobbled together the town folks in the southern part of the province with the rural people to the north. Those country folks were the real "Galatians," which is the English transliteration of the Greek word for what the Romans called the *Keltoi*, or the Celts.

Although the Celts are most often associated with Britain and Ireland, the Celtic civilization stretched across northern Europe and represented an alternative to the ordered, logical way of life of the Romans. The Celts were a fierce, warlike, passionate people. They stripped naked when they went to war. They placed the heads of their opponents on poles. They worshiped the sun and honored oak groves as sacred. Storytellers were held in high honor. The Celts were advanced scientifically (They used salt to cure hams and created vivid dyes.); but because they did not have a written language, the Greeks and Romans thought of them as ignorant barbarians (*barbaroi*, so called because Greek speakers disdained all other languages as nonsense syllables: *bar bar bar*).

The Celtic gods were not isolated on a lofty Mount Olympus. Because the Celts believed that the thin line between the human and the divine realms was easily crossed, the idea of Emmanuel, God With Us, uniquely present in Jesus, was easy for them to accept.

Paul shared with the Galatians the good news that "you are Abraham's descendants, heirs according to the promise" (Galatians 3:29) without having to behave like the people of other cultures. Paul was afraid the Celts might lose their new identity because of interference from other believers.

About the Scripture

## You Are There!

For the Celts, the stories of their mythology were not descriptions of something that had happened in the distant past. They believed in a mystic sense that these events were a present part of their reality. So when Paul told the Jesus story, it was as real to them as if they had seen the events with their own eyes. Paul could not help but cry out in frustration to the Galatians, who having become eyewitnesses then denied the evidence of their own eyes, "You irrational Galatians [or Celts]!... Jesus Christ was put on display as crucified before your eyes!" (Galatians 3:1).

Some faiths are tied to a particular culture and language. That's not the case with faith in Jesus. We are comfortable with the idea that African, Indonesian, Latin American, Native American, and North American Christians, among others, bring their unique personalities to worship. Paul was content that Jewish Christians like him could remain ethnically Jewish. But he also felt that members of the larger Greco-Roman world should remain Greco-Roman and the Celtic believers should remain Celts while all proclaimed Christ. These people did not need to become Jewish in order to be Christian.

So the Celts did actually remain Celts ethnically. That's why the Celtic cross featured a prominent circle. Celts recognized the sun as the source of all life. The circle, a symbol of the sun, is prominently featured in Celtic art. By placing the circle in the cross (and often including an incident from the life of Jesus artistically represented in that circle), Celts transferred their image of the source of all life from the sun to the cross.

Part of the Letter to the Galatians' central message for our time is that it is not God's will that we become an ethnically pure, homogeneous fellowship of believers—not in Paul's day and not now. We are what we are. The heavenly vision of "a great crowd...from every nation, tribe, people, and language" (Revelation 7:9) is hard to maintain, but it is hard work worth doing!

*How It Works*

My first congregation was about half African American, half white, with a smattering of Asians and two Hispanics (the organist and I). Our life as a church was not always an easy one. Something as simple as a potluck meal was complicated by our different senses of time, event, duration, dress, and address (Was I "Frank," "Pastor Frank," or "Reverend Ramirez"?). It took work, but it was worth it.

The Celts of Galatia felt outside pressure to conform ethnically. Perhaps some gave in, which is why Paul wondered why they were "so quickly deserting the one who called you by the grace of Christ to follow another gospel" (Galatians 1:6). This, of course, was not really another gospel. Specifically, there were those who wished to enslave the Galatians to their interpretation of the Bible, which is why Paul ironically turned the tables on the troublemakers when he used a story from the Hebrew Scriptures involving Abraham, Sarah, and Hagar to affirm the Celts' ethnic status.

Across the Testaments

### The Tables Are Turned

In Galatians 4:21–5:1, Paul uses the story of Abraham, Sarah, and Hagar from Genesis (16:1-15; 18:1-15; 21:1-20) to describe the Celts and the Jewish Christians; but in an ironic twist, he switches the roles. The Celts are represented by Sarah's child ("You are children of the promise like Isaac" [4:28].), he insists. The irony is further compounded because those who use the Hebrew Scriptures to exclude are represented as the descendants of the slave woman Hagar. This would have startled Paul's first listeners, perhaps in the same way that some people react when I insist that immigrants, documented or undocumented, exemplify what is truly American a lot more than some native-born citizens, themselves the descendants of immigrants. Immigrants are the ones who believe in the American dream enough to act on it.

The timeline surrounding Paul's visits to the Celts is a little muddy. The Book of Acts records a trip through the southern part of Galatia on Paul's first missionary journey (see Acts 13:13–14:7). During that trip he was harassed by those who insisted Gentile Christians needed to become ethnically Jewish by adopting circumcision and observing specific Jewish holidays.

The crisis culminated in the Jerusalem Council (see Acts 15:1-29 and Galatians 2:1-10), which some think took place around A.D. 48. This helps us to date the Letter to the Galatians at around the year 51 or 52.

The council seemed to settle the matter. Faith in Christ, not cultural practice, makes us right with God. Christians, therefore, were not required to adopt the ethnic backgrounds of other Christians.

Paul then journeyed to the churches to explain the decision. This journey may have taken him through ethnically Celtic northern Galatia (Acts 16:6). His reasons for stopping, though, were medical, not theological. Paul's severe illness and the Celts' hospitality led to a bond so strong that Paul seems to have felt personally betrayed by their straying, which led to this letter.

About the Scripture

## Celtic Medicine and Hospitality

Paul was at pains to make it clear that his first visit with the Celts was an accident. "You know that I first preached the gospel to you because of an illness" (Galatians 4:13). The fact that the Galatians would have "dug out" their eyes to give them to Paul (4:15) suggests he may have had an eye ailment, possibly a disgusting abscess. In the Gospels, those who were ill were isolated from the healthy; but the Celts, for all their ferocity, were a passionately hospitable people and would not have isolated Paul. Some think that the apostle may have bathed his eyes in the warm springs of the spas in the Galatian territory while he, a total stranger, was cared for by the Celts.

The Galatians strayed from the revealed gospel. This led to one of the most extended biographical statements on Paul's part (Galatians 1:10–2:14).

In describing his conversion, transformed from enemy of God to apostle, Paul was at pains to emphasize that the revelation came from Jesus (Galatians 1:12), which is why he asserted that he had little contact with the other apostles in Jerusalem (1:17) other than a short visit three years after his conversion (1:18). So great was Paul's transformation that some Christians remained skeptical.

*Biblical Sanitizer*

One of the issues at the heart of the problem Paul was addressing was the matter of clean and unclean. We are not talking about whether one uses hand sanitizer. In every culture there are some things people do and some things people don't do. There are things people eat and things people don't eat. In some African cultures, for instance, the left hand is never used for eating because it is reserved for hygienic purposes. In our culture we don't eat dogs or horses, but in other places they do. There are Asian cultures that despise cheese. I remember the disdain displayed by some European guests at our table (They quickly tried to hide it.) because we served corn for dinner, which one of their children referred to as "pig food."

There may be nothing wrong with the food in question, but our minds can make it unpalatable. I recall my older sister turning as green as the guacamole at the Gomez family picnic when she discovered there was tongue in it.

Gentiles (including the Celts) and Jews considered the others' foods unclean. They also had different views on male circumcision. Jews practiced it as a sign of God's covenant with Abraham. Greeks looked on the practice as barbaric mutilation. Unity was not easy to achieve.

Hard work is required to get past some of our prejudices. Thirty years ago when I was in seminary, there was a Korean family in our housing unit who made kim chee during the winter. I am ashamed to say that when we smelled it cooking, some of us thought a plumbing disaster had taken place. The cabbage dish (which is served with every meal) is very strong because it is buried in jars to ferment. Now I like it. At the time, I said some ignorant things.

In an empire where people did not cross economic, gender, educational, and cultural lines to eat together, Christians broke all the rules by eating at a common table. This radical behavior caused great suspicion. Rumors abounded about Christians.

In A.D. 115, Pliny the Younger, who was governor of Pontus and Bithynia from 111–113, wrote to the emperor Trajan about his investigation into the supposedly bizarre practices of the Christians. All he could report was that they rose before dawn, ate a meal together, and sang a hymn to Christ as to a god. His source for this information was two female deacons, both slaves, whom he tortured to make sure they were telling the truth.[1] This clearly demonstrates how economic and gender lines were crossed at the Christian table.

Table fellowship is extraordinarily important for Christians. We bless each other with the gift of acceptance. We have one table. That's why it was ironic when peer pressure caused Peter to back away from eating with those these troublemakers considered unclean (Galatians 2:11-14). Peter was the one who had baptized a Roman centurion some years before and said at the time, "I really am learning that God doesn't show partiality to one group of people over another" (Acts 10:34). Paul might have been quoting him when he wrote, "God doesn't show favoritism" (Galatians 2:6).

Note that Paul did not reject Judaism; he himself maintained his cultural practices. But no ethnic practice is essential to Christian faith.

So what is the value of the Hebrew Bible? Paul says it was not meant to create boundaries to exclude others. The Old Testament is a *paidagogos*—an instructor who is a slave but who is the master over the student for a time. However, once the child who is tutored comes to maturity, "we are no longer under a custodian. For you are all God's children through faith in Christ Jesus" (Galatians 3:25-26). As mature members of one family, we are now equals.

Paul told the Galatians they should stay Celtic. He would remain Jewish. I am certain he would tell us today that Irish American Christians should stay that way; and the same goes for African American Christians, Italian American Christians, German American Christians—well, you get the idea. According to humorist Garrison Keillor, the town motto for all the folks who live in his mythical Lake Wobegon is *Sumus Quod Sumus:* "We Are Who We Are." This is worth celebrating. We all should enjoy and celebrate what is best in each other, enjoying, learning, sharing. "For you are all God's children through faith in Christ Jesus" (Galatians 3:26).

Was Paul serious? He was serious enough to tell a real, honest-to-goodness one of the twelve original apostles to pick up his lunch tray and move back to the Gentile table. That's why Paul confronted Peter in front of everybody. This adherence to an incorrect interpretation of the Hebrew Scriptures was wrong, wrong, wrong.

Paul's letter to the Celts is crucial to our understanding of salvation by grace. But if it's what you believe, not what you do, that matters, why did Paul take Peter to task for what he was *doing* instead of what he *believed*? We're saved by grace, not works, aren't we? Maybe Paul reprimanded Peter because we can say "Jesus is Lord" all we want; but if we really believe, our faith will result in action.

Paul, for all that he championed the right of other ethnic and cultural believers to maintain their outlooks and practices, was profoundly Hebraic in his thinking. The Hebrew language did not support abstract thought the way the Greek language did. Faith in Christ is what we do, not what we say we believe.

Are we really one in Christ? One of the things I've noticed in churches is that folks like to stick with their friends, whether it is in conversation before and after church, the choice of where they sit during worship or at meals, or in their associations in the workaday world. It's just easier, sitting with someone we know, talking about stuff we like or have in common.

The Letter to the Galatians is a passionate letter for a passionate people. The Christian community is not Jewish, Greek, or Celtic. Jews, Greeks, and Celts all belong. So do you. So do I.

## Live the Story

One of my proudest moments came when I was pastoring that little black-and-white congregation in Los Angeles. It was when we invited the new Korean-speaking fellowship over for a joint potluck. The tables were loaded with exotic dishes. The palates of folks from both churches were challenged. The children gravitated to the food they ate at home, but the adults from both congregations made it a point to dish up big helpings of stuff they had never eaten. That was the clearest message we could have given to each other that we were one family in Christ.

Our faith is about moving beyond our comfort zones. Make it a point to get out of your tracks and widen the circle. Sit with someone different, approach newcomers and act as a guide during worship, eat with everyone, challenge yourself at the church potluck to be with others. Don't just talk. Do.

Describe your faith in one sentence.

Describe who you are. What is the intersection of your identity and your faith?

What is your experience in other cultures? What challenges have you faced in working with others with different backgrounds?

Make a statement about belief in Jesus. Is that statement tied to cultural assumptions? Take time now to pray that we may be one in Christ while remaining who we are.

1. From *The Letters of the Younger Pliny*, translated by Betty Radice (Penguin Books, 1969); pages 293–295.

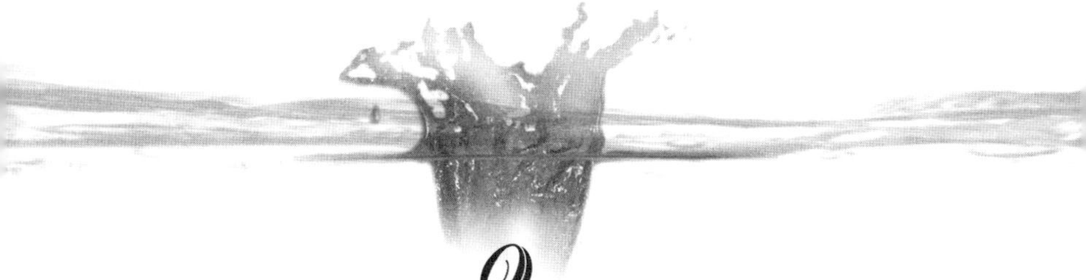

# 2.

# Free to Be One in Christ

*Galatians 5:13–6:18*

## Claim Your Story

The teacher told my dad he could attend the little school in Fierro, New Mexico, if he learned English. So he did. Later, while serving in the US Navy, in response to the mocking of his fellow sailors, he removed all traces of his accent. That's why we Ramirez children have no accent. Some of our cousins wonder what's wrong with us.

"English only" laws bug me, but I suppose we Hispanics should feel honored. Others have been the target of suspicion as well. During World War I the hostility against German Americans was so intense, people stopped speaking German in church! Lutherans, Brethren, and Mennonites dropped German hymns and prayers.

In Galatians we learn that we fulfill God's law by loving our neighbors as ourselves. Leviticus goes even further: We are also to love the alien as ourselves!

For a nation that prides itself on diversity, why do some people seem to think we all ought to look and act the same? Does this thinking infect the church? Why, or why not?

How narrowly do you define your neighbor? Which ethnic group have you been suspicious of during times of crisis?

How much do people have to act like you for you to accept them? What does any of this have to do with serving Jesus?

Across the Testaments

### Love Who?

When Paul told the Galatians that the whole law is summed up in the command *"Love your neighbor as yourself"* (5:14), he was quoting both Leviticus 19:18 and the words of Jesus. Jesus quoted the verse from Leviticus when he had a dispute with the religious authorities (Matthew 22:34-40). The nineteenth chapter of this often unread book (Leviticus) is a practical guide to fulfilling the law, and we'll have cause to refer to it again later in this study. For now, it is enough to know that there's another verse in the chapter that bookends nicely with the one we just quoted. Some have called it the most radical saying not only in the Bible, but in the ancient world. It's not just our neighbor whom we're to love. This passage also insists, "Any immigrant who lives with you must be treated as if they were one of your citizens. You must love them as yourself" (Leviticus 19:34).

## Enter the Bible Story

*Read the Instructions*

*The Greatest American Hero* was an old 1980s TV superhero series with a twist. Space aliens gave a special-education teacher a suit that gave him superpowers. The only problem was, the teacher lost the instruction manual and had a hard time controlling his powers. He didn't so much fly as flail wildly through the air.

The problem for the Galatians was not that they lost the instructions; they were forced to choose between not one, but two very different manuals.

One manual was brought by missionaries from the Jerusalem church. They had come to visit these Celts (the Galatians; see Chapter 1), who were new Christians, and told them it was not enough to believe in Jesus as Lord. The missionaries from the Jerusalem church dumped the whole law book in their laps and then told them to memorize everything and be ready for a test real soon. Until the Celts passed, they wouldn't qualify as Christians in the eyes of the believers from Jerusalem.

We do not know just how official this delegation from Jerusalem was, but it must have had enough authority to make the Galatians doubt themselves. They didn't know what to think.

Now who would want to argue with the assertion that the instruction manual for Christians is the Bible? Remember, the New Testament hadn't been written. The Bible for the first Christians was the Hebrew Scriptures. The trouble was, these Scriptures could be confusing, perplexing, even obscure in places. What did it all mean?

So Paul gave the Galatians the real instruction manual. It was simple: "All the Law has been fulfilled in a single statement: *Love your neighbor as yourself*" (5:14). Paul was quoting both Jesus and Leviticus 19:18.

The apostle reminded the Galatians that they were called to freedom. They were no longer slaves to sin. Instead, through love they could become slaves to each other. Become slaves voluntarily? Be conquered by love? Crazy? Maybe. But it just might work.

Even so, Paul believed that the law was a positive thing. It wasn't meant to be a chain confining God's people. The apostle's Jerusalem opponents believed the law was a precise set of instructions that must be followed in detail. Every single bit of it had to be done exactly right. Paul knew that was impossible. Yet he agreed the law was divinely inspired and infallible. How could Paul hold these two seemingly opposing viewpoints?

The clue to this paradox lies in understanding Galatians 5:16: "I say be guided by the Spirit." Think of the Bible as a map, not an instruction manual, that guides us on the journey but allows us to walk at our own pace. By following this guide, the Galatians wouldn't need to lose their ethnic identity in order to follow Christ.

What it comes down to is this: Doing the law is impossible. Fulfilling the law is accomplished by loving each other.

Even though this particular controversy was outwardly about circumcision, it was really about power. Love and power are two different things. Loving each other means letting us remain who we are ethnically, culturally, personally. To be transformed in Christ is to have our old life baptized.

*Then and Now*

I come from a big city you may have heard of: Los Angeles. Yet as I write this, I am serving a church in sparsely populated Bedford County, Pennsylvania. Hunting is so important in this culture that the first day of deer season is a school holiday. Although I'd never hunted before, or even owned a gun, I instantly realized how integral this practice was to the culture. In this area, moms teach their sons and dads teach their daughters responsible gun ownership. The meat that is harvested feeds families all winter. So the very first year I served that church, I organized a special blessing for the hunters on the Sunday after Thanksgiving (the day before deer season opened). I've repeated it every year since.

Some of my friends out west grimaced when I described the service, and a few even questioned how one could be a Christian and hunt (For them the sound of gunfire meant trouble, not dinner.). Paul knew the Galatians needed to remain Galatians, the Ephesians should remain Ephesians, and the Philippians had to stay Philippians—and folks from Bloody Run are going to stay folks from Bloody Run. All can honor Jesus Christ just as they are.

So, loving our neighbor as our self sets us free. But what does having that freedom mean? Does it mean having the freedom to do whatever we feel like? Possibly, but not sensibly. The baseball great Mickey Mantle came from a family in which the men died young. As a result, he lived his life riotously, risking his health while using his freedom to do whatever he wanted. In his old age, his health deteriorated as the result of his choices. He freely admitted that if he'd known he was going to live so long, he might have been more careful.

Freedom is not about just doing what we want. That's why Paul wrote, "Don't let this freedom be an opportunity to indulge your selfish impulses, but serve each other through love" (Galatians 5:13). We are not to use our freedom for giving in to our worst impulses.

If we do that—well, this is one of the most striking parts of Paul's letter—"if you bite and devour each other, be careful that you don't get eaten up by each other!" (Galatians 5:15). This reminds me of the time we walked across the border from Columbus, New Mexico, to Palomas,

About the Scripture

### Ground Control

"Don't let this freedom be an opportunity to indulge your selfish impulses" (Galatians 5:13).

The Greek word *aphorme*, translated as "opportunity," was the word in classical Greek for a staging area for a military operation, the spot where you'd funnel supplies before setting out on an expedition. What is translated as "selfish impulses" is literally "flesh" but doesn't refer to the physical body; it refers to the worst of our impulses. I'd translate this phrase as, "Don't let your freedom become a staging area for an assault by your worst impulses."

Mexico. We wanted to buy some Mexican vanilla (It's just better.), the kind of soap my dad likes, and some handmade nativity sets for Christmas gifts. At first, we were having a good time; but off to our right was a short, squat building from which came the sound of cheers. I was horrified to realize animal fighting was going on there.

Animals are taught to fight like humans in those staged fights. In the real world, animals may fight for territory or mates; but their fights consist of swagger and noise and a few passes until the superiority of one or the other is established, after which the other backs off. Animals don't naturally fight to the death, but we teach them to fight like humans. Although Paul in this verse uses the image of people fighting like dogs, I have to argue that it's people who fight until there is nothing left. This is not how we love each other.

*So How Come?*

The reason Paul used this image was that this vicious fighting was a characteristic of the Celts, who were such fearsome warriors they frightened the Roman legions. The Romans fought in formation, using tactics and logic. Celtic warriors observed no order in battle, threw off their clothes, screamed full-throated cries, and thrust themselves on their opponents without regard for their own survival.

Celts also practiced sorcery, and you will notice that among the behaviors Paul listed to avoid were some of the worst behaviors of the Celts (see Galatians 5:19-21). Lists of bad behaviors were common in the ancient world for both Jew and Gentile. The fact that "casting spells" and "fighting" made this list makes it likely that, as we suggested in the first chapter, Paul was addressing Celts.

Walking in the Spirit holds these worst desires in check. Why? Because when we walk in the Spirit, we're doing something, something positive like, well, cultivating fruit!

That leads to Paul's famous passage about the fruit of the Spirit (Galatians 5:22-23). I like this image because it suggests not necessarily what we will do every time but, in the words of the Quakers, which way we want to lean. Fruit must be planted, tended, cultivated, and patiently waited for. There are weeds to be pulled, compost to be formed, and mulch to lay down. We can't guarantee that every year will be a good one for the fruit. There may be a late frost, or the tree may be a little tired. Yet if we do "not get tired of doing good,...in time we'll have a harvest if we don't give up" (6:9). The important thing is to lay the foundation, to cultivate good fruit.

We may still come across something wild and unplanned. In the wild patch that borders my simple acre, I sometimes find persistent weeds like burdock that choke off other plants. But I also find wild berries and volunteer asparagus, and that's a wonderful grace. Grace is also there when we fail. An isolated sin may not be indicative of who we are. God knows this. Like Paul says, "Make no mistake, God is not mocked" (Galatians 6:7). God knows who we really are.

The fruit of the Spirit includes "love, joy, peace, patience, kindness, goodness, faithfulness, gentleness, and self control" (Galatians 5:22-23). Here Paul makes a second, shocking statement that must have knocked the Galatians off their moorings. Earlier he had told them to enslave themselves to each other in love (We'll talk more about slavery in a later chapter.). Now we learn that nurturing these good things means crucifying our worst desires in Christ Jesus (5:24). Crucifixion was so horrible, so obscene, so impossible to watch, that it did not appear in Christian art for five centuries, until that method of execution was no longer used.

Actually, that's not exactly correct. There is one depiction of the crucifixion of Jesus Christ, possibly from the second or third century. It's a piece of graffiti on the wall of a guardroom on the Palatine Hill near the Circus Maximus in Rome. It shows a man with a donkey's head hanging on a cross, with a slave at his feet, his arm raised in homage, with the mocking caption, "Alexamenos worships [his] god." Evidently one slave mocked another for honoring Jesus. Crucifying our old life leaves us open to disdain.

*Tying It All Together*

The final verses of the letter seem to be a series of short statements that occurred to Paul, who was apparently dictating this letter, as he closed. These are things that are self-evidently true but need saying once in a while. Two of the items are even contradictory. Paul reminded the Galatians to "carry each other's burdens and so you will fulfill the law of Christ" (6:2), that law of loving each other that is so essential to our life together. But almost immediately Paul also said, "Each person will have to carry their own load" (6:5). This is a great example of how biblical wisdom asks us to evaluate our present situation. There are times when we have to bear each other's burdens, but there are also times when it's important for us to carry our own load. It just depends.

Paul's intent was to encourage the Celts to worship Jesus in ways consistent with their culture. He wanted them to be Celts. The Celts baptized their worship of the sun and placed that circle in their stone crosses. They were healers, so the stories of Jesus as a healer made lots of sense to them.

Think about different churches you have visited and the different ways Christ has been honored. You may have sung different hymns. Different stories may have been depicted in the stained-glass windows, or the windows may have been clear glass. Whether hands are waved about vigorously or rest folded in a lap, whether piano and organ are played or there's a guitar band with drums, Paul would be pleased as long as Jesus Christ is proclaimed as Lord!

About the Scripture

### Cipherin'

"Look at the large letters I'm making with my own handwriting!" (Galatians 6:11). The printed word looks so definitive on a page between professionally designed covers that we can sometimes forget there's a process involved in bringing us the message. Just as there was a time before the age of personal computing when keyboard skills were not universally required or attained, so too, for thousands of years, literate people did not necessarily have the skills to write down their words on papyrus. They often relied on professionals to do it for them. Paul could apparently draw letters, but they were large and ungainly. They were, in effect, his signature; but they cause us to ask, Did Paul dictate this letter word for word? Did he write out a draft to be copied by a professional scribe? Or did the believer who took dictation have a hand in the exact phrasing of this important letter?

To worship in ways consistent with who you are requires that you love yourself and love the God who made you who you are. Remember the verse Paul quoted. It's no good loving your neighbor as yourself if you don't love yourself. Take care of yourself. Use your freedom to make better choices. Honor God whether it is by hunting, playing bridge, writing poetry, planting a garden, kissing a baby, or cooking a meal.

Do not use this freedom to retreat into fear and lies, however. The delegation from Jerusalem mistakenly tried to lure the Galatians back to a past that never was. Love God. Love yourself as much as you deserve, as much as God loves you. And, of course, as slaves ready to wash each other's feet, love each other as fiercely as you love yourselves.

## Live the Story

It was nearly fifty years ago, but I still remember with both a faint smile and a grimace my dad's attempt to grow a new lawn. A neighbor boy deliberately stomped across the fragile seedlings. When challenged by my father to walk around rather than across the lawn, he arrogantly replied,

About the Christian Faith

## Just Plain Different

The Jerusalem Christians weren't the only ones who were exasperated with the Celtic Christians for not conforming to their idea of proper practice. The Roman church of the seventh century was just as frustrated with the Irish church for its insistence on following its own practices, especially in the matter of the date of Easter. The calculations for the date of the holiday were designed to pinpoint the date of the Passover, which was based on a lunar calendar, and bring it into line with the solar calendar in use by the Christians. At the Council of Nicea in 325, the Christian church took into account the major calendar reforms of the Roman Empire in establishing the date of Easter, but the Irish Christians were not in attendance and did not know about these reforms—all of which suggests that the Celtic Christianity Paul established on his trips through Galatia had crossed the channel into Britain and Ireland long before Saint Patrick came to the Emerald Isle.

"It's a free country." Dad knew better than to argue with a six-year-old, but he did take a moment to talk to us about what freedom really means.

Paul told the Galatians not to let their freedom become a staging ground for the worst of their desires but an opportunity to be slaves for each other. In the end, freedom is about what we *get* to do for each other, not what we *have* to do.

What do you get to do for Jesus? If you are reading this chapter as a member of a group, what do you get to do for the other members?

How does our freedom in Christ help us to love each other?

What does freedom mean for you? What sort of limits are you free to set for other people? What challenges are you free to face together as the people of Christ?

What will you do with your freedom in Christ?

# 3.

# One of the Above

*Ephesians 1–3*

## Claim Your Story

I used to see this old, beat-up car that doubled as an evangelistic billboard. Every inch was plastered with Bible verses, Christian sayings, and warnings—mostly warnings. Every inch of that car was dedicated to the message that we're all sinners and unless we straighten up and fly right, we're all going straight to hell.

Which is all true. But I had to wonder if the driver turned off more folks than he attracted to the Word of God. There seems to be this belief that there's only one way to share the message. Paul knew better. He did not drive some old beater plastered with bumper stickers into Ephesus. His message was tailored for each audience. It was the same gospel, the same good news, of course, but told in a way people of each particular culture could understand.

God is love. We all believe that. Can you think of ways your actions and attitude express precisely the opposite?

When in your experience have Christians through unChristlike actions divided believers into different camps rather than uniting all in praise?

When has your insistence on having your own way meant that no way is what you got?

## Enter the Bible Story

*Introducing the Letter to the Ephesians*

A couple of days before I officiated at the wedding of my oldest son, Francisco, and his fiancée, Margaret, my brand new ten-year old grandson,

José, asked me to write a poem for him to read during the ceremony. I gladly obliged. *Ahora mi familia son del mundo*, I began, swiftly penning a fourteen-line sonnet that mixed Spanish and English to celebrate that "now my family is of the world." Since most in attendance were bilingual, I felt confident they'd understand the poem.

The poem I wrote for another wedding was totally different because almost everyone there spoke only English. The fact is, I usually tailor my writing for the audience. I'm the same person, but I use a different vocabulary and style depending on the occasion.

I mention this because some question the authorship of Ephesians because it has a different vocabulary and style than some of Paul's other letters. As a writer I respond, "So?" Paul didn't change his message, but he did change his style. As we have seen, Galatians was written to a largely Celtic population (see Chapter 1). Philippi, we will discover, was a colony of Rome and filtered life through a Roman perspective. What about the Ephesians?

Ephesus was one of the most important cities of Asia Minor, an ancient city that became part of the Roman Empire in 133 B.C. At the time, its

About the Scripture

## Please Mr. Postman

So to whom was the Letter to the Ephesians addressed? The Christians in Ephesus, of course. Right? Well, maybe. The oldest manuscripts do not include an addressee, almost as if it was intentionally left blank. And some think it odd that even though Paul spent three years in Ephesus, he wrote as though he didn't know the people that well (see 1:15; 3:1-7). Some speculate this is really the letter to the Laodiceans referred to in Colossians 4:16, a group of people with many similarities to the Ephesians. Others point out that Paul's letters were probably shared among congregations. Perhaps the addressee was dropped when it was copied. Since a few ancient manuscripts also drop "Rome" from the Letter to the Romans, this may not have been such an uncommon practice.

location at the mouth of the River Cayster made it an important trade center. Ironically, after the harbor was narrowed to improve navigation, the port became silted; and today the ruins of Ephesus are six miles inland.

Ephesus was a center for many faiths, including mystery religions as well as the cult of emperor worship. Most residents of this proud, sophisticated, and ancient city had a fierce nationalistic pride centered around the worship of the goddess Artemis. Her temple in Ephesus was one of the seven wonders of the ancient world.

The Ephesians' pride and satisfaction in their way of life may have played a role when Paul was nearly lynched at a mock trial conducted in the outdoor theater (an architectural marvel that held over 24,000 people). Paul had resided in Ephesus for over 2 years, and his ministry had made such an impact that the economy of the region was threatened (see Acts 19:21-40). That is, the magic "industry" was an important part of the local economy. As a result of Paul's preaching, many people were converted and then burned their books of magic. Silversmiths feared that further conversions would also impact the thriving souvenir industry (They sold miniature copies of the temple of Artemis.). So the artisans took advantage of the hostility between Jews and Gentiles as an excuse to haul Paul before the mob in the theater. Only when the town clerk warned the crowd that any civil unrest would attract the unwelcome interest of Rome was Paul released, unharmed.

After his adventures in Ephesus, Paul passed through Macedonia to Jerusalem, where he was once more arrested on false charges. Fearing death at the hands of the mob, he appealed to Caesar. This led to his imprisonment in Rome while he waited for the case to be heard. So, imprisoned in Rome (and depending on which imprisonment we're talking about, the book may have been written around A.D. 60 or 64), Paul wrote to the Ephesian Christians to demonstrate that the peace of Christ would create peace between Jew and Gentile and all humanity.

### *Real Peace*

The letter begins with the apostle's typical wish of "Grace and peace" (Ephesians 1:2). This greeting combined the standard Greek letter open-

About the Scripture

### Take a Letter, Please

When we talk about Paul writing a letter, we often picture him at a desk, pen in hand, and a sheet of papyrus spread out before him. However, Paul may have dictated his letters; and there's no better illustration of that than the fact that Ephesians 1:3-14 is actually one long run-on sentence. So is 1:15-23. The CEB rightfully breaks the first passage into twelve shorter sentences and the second passage into seven to make it easier for us to understand.

ing wish for good health (The words for "health" and "grace" or "gift" are very similar.) and the standard Hebrew letter opening wish for "shalom," which means both peace and health. This peace comes from "God our Father and our Lord Jesus Christ" (1:2).

This was a crucial difference from the understanding most Ephesians held. One of the reasons many worshiped the emperor as a god was because of the belief that he was the source of peace. The Roman Empire forced an uneasy peace by preventing ethnic groups from fighting. But Paul believed Jesus was (and is) the real peacemaker. The peace of Christ that Paul presents is more profound. Christ made peace by reconciling all ethnic groups into one family.

When Paul states that "God chose us in Christ to be holy" (Ephesians 1:4), he is alluding to the command of Leviticus 19:2 that all the people will be holy for God is holy. As Paul makes clear, this new relationship among all peoples was not an improvisation on the part of God. Paul apparently believed it was predestined that this would happen.

The mystery religions referred to earlier trafficked in "secret knowledge." Only slowly, after long study and by progressing through layer after layer toward the ultimate inner circle, was one initiated into the mysteries that were hidden from the larger population. But "God revealed his hidden design to us, which is according to his goodwill and the plan that he intended to accomplish through his Son" (Ephesians 1:9). This mystery

Across the Testaments

## Holy, Holy, Holy

"To the holy and faithful people in Christ Jesus in Ephesus" (Ephesians 1:1).

The Hebraic understanding of holy was not to be found in an attitude but in action. This holiness code is best expressed in the verse "You must be holy, because I, the LORD your God, am holy" (Leviticus 19:2). The Leviticus chapter goes on to define the condition of being holy by the imperatives to maintain honest weights, to pay workers on time and according to contract, to set aside a portion of the harvest for the poor, and to love both your neighbor and the alien as yourself. *Holy living is holy action,* 24/7, not just on the sabbath. The command in Leviticus 19 is for all of Israel to be holy. Paul states that now all nations are included in the definition of holy!

was not really hidden. It had been revealed in plain sight, not just to the initiates, but to the whole world through the resurrection of Jesus Christ. Jesus is "far above every ruler and authority and power and angelic power" (1:21); it was (and is) there for all to see.

We all have a share in the resurrection of Jesus. It has happened because of God's mercy, God's initiative, God's grace. I think the Common English Bible has captured the original Greek perfectly: "You are saved by God's grace because of your faith. This salvation is God's gift. It's not something you possessed. It's not something you did that you can be proud of. Instead, we are God's accomplishment" (Ephesians 2:8-10).

This is "the climax of all times" (Ephesians 1:10). If Paul seems to speak of predestination, it is a predestination that is not about individuals. God has predestined all of creation—including all people—to be a part of his righteousness.

Many years ago, there was a popular Christian bumper sticker that read simply, "I Found It!" If you were asked what it meant, you were supposed to explain, "I found Jesus." But a better bumper sticker, one consistent with the Letter to the Ephesians, would have read, "He Found Us!"

The cross has broken down all the barriers that made us foreigners to each other. This was not easy. Take the issue of circumcision, which was important in Paul's day. Jews considered circumcision essential to membership in God's family. Gentiles saw it as barbaric mutilation. Both considered the other unclean. The cross changed everything. Thanks to the blood of Christ, "you who once were so far away have been brought near" (Ephesians 2:13).

### *Spirit of the Age*

This new situation creates its own problems. As long as we are separated from each other, we can dismiss each other as enemies. We can believe half-truths and misconceptions. But families have to learn to live together. Christians, regardless of background, are all part of the same household. There will be more about the Roman household in the next chapter. Suffice it to say for now that it was hard for the Ephesian Christians to get along then. It's hard for us now.

God's grace, Paul wrote, has saved us all from a cosmic condition. He alluded to the "destructive spiritual power" (Ephesians 2:2), sometimes translated as "powers of the air." It was believed that the air below the heavens was ruled by the spirit of the age—in other words, by demonic forces. These forces defined the way people thought; and as Paul states, this is a toxic, false way to look at things.

We, too, can become prisoners of the age. We speak of eras and ages in different ways, referring to the 50s, or the 60s, or the Me Generation, Generation X, the Sandwich Generation, and so on in ways that define us and confine us. What chance do we have against these spirits of the air?

Fortunately, "God is rich in mercy" (Ephesians 2:4). This made the cross the pivot of history, the turning point. Salvation by grace is a combination of faith *and* works. Salvation leads us to do good things. I'm reminded of Eliza Doolittle's frustrated plea in the musical *My Fair Lady*, where she demands that a young man no longer talk of love but, as she says, "*Show me*."

The language toward the end of Ephesians 2, about God building a new temple—a new building that we're all a part of—is in direct contrast to both the backdrop of the emperor worship, which was empty and could accomplish nothing, and the worship in the Temple of Jerusalem.

That latter temple was a building of barriers. There was a stark warning at the edge of the public portion telling Gentiles to proceed no farther on pain of death. Beyond that, there were barriers first to women, then to all men except priests, and then to all priests but the High Priest.

This new temple, which was made up of the Ephesians themselves, had Christ Jesus as the cornerstone. "Christ is building you into a place where God lives through the Spirit" (Ephesians 2:22).

That's true now as well. In our society we love to exclude. Some people act as if they're more American than others. Even though we're a nation of immigrants, some despise the next set of immigrants. It can be worse in the church. Some Christians like to say, "God has no grandchildren" because we're all adopted children of God. Despite this, there are those who act as if they were the proprietors of the body of Christ. Newcomers are welcome to sit in some other pew and contribute to the offering, but only as long as they behave and do what they're told. They are not allowed to be leaders, and their ideas are dismissed out of hand.

I remember an odd incident I witnessed in another church, long ago. A relatively new member, who was part of a different ethnic group than the older members of that congregation, was elected chair of the church board. A descendant of one of the church's founders felt threatened and announced to this new board chair that the real power in the church was in the board of directors. They made all the real decisions; the board chair didn't matter.

In fact, the board of directors consisted of five people whose only duty was to meet for five minutes once a year as the technical owners of the facility, which they owned in the name of the district office. But that wasn't the point. It was uncomfortable to the old guard when those so very far away had been brought near by the blood of Christ.

Paul responded in a way that's staggering; but because of our own cultural preconceptions, we don't realize what he was saying. "This is why

I kneel before the Father," he wrote (Ephesians 3:14). Because some of us kneel in prayer, we think that's what Paul was talking about. But Jewish prayer was performed standing, with arms outstretched in what is called the *orante* position; so Paul was not talking about prayer.

In Hebraic thought, kneeling was an act of awe. It occurred when one was so "jelly-legged" in the presence of the divine that one lost the ability to stand.

What was so awe inspiring that Paul collapsed into a kneeling position? Simply this: "Every ethnic group in heaven or on earth is recognized by him" (Ephesians 3:15). No one is a stranger to God. There are no outsiders anymore.

Paul was hoping that we'll experience the same awe when he added, "I ask that you'll have the power to grasp love's width and length, height and depth, together with all believers" (Ephesians 3:18). The apostle prayed that we'll all come to know the love of Christ.

About the Christian Faith

## For Personal Use Only

The first half of Ephesians ends with a doxology (3:20-21), a Greek term that means literally "word of glory." A doxology is a climax of worship, praising God for his power, for his action among us, for the very fact of his existence. This doxology ties the church from all generations together with Jesus Christ in eternal praise.

Ironically, the most famous doxology was written not for corporate worship, but for individual devotions. Thomas Ken insisted his hymn "Awake My Soul and With the Sun" (published in 1674) be sung only for private devotions in one's room and not in public worship. He lived in an era when the only acceptable hymns were based directly on Scripture, especially psalms. Hymns as we know them were not allowed. Yet the doxology stanza of this ten-stanza hymn, which drew all of creation and all the hosts of heaven together in glorious praise, is better known and sung more in church than any other hymn! Many Christians know it by heart:

Praise God from whom all blessings flow;
Praise him all creatures here below;
Praise him above ye heavenly hosts;
Praise Father, Son, and Holy Ghost.

False mysteries are always popping up, with one new theological fad coming after another. Despite the fact that there are many confusing choices on the menu, we are called to make a decision. It's tempting to say that we want all the above; but for Christians, as the Ephesians were told, it has to be just one of the above: Jesus.

How would you define the spirit of our age? How does it influence us? Does it influence us for good or for evil?

What fads and false mysteries that you recall have influenced the church? How did people react?

## Live the Story

It's been decades since I went to seminary. I know there are boxes full of notes from those days stored away in the garage, but I've never looked at them. It's funny what I do use: the stories the professors told. One of my professors at Bethany Theological Seminary told a great one about the old man who hated everyone and Christians most of all. Then one day he fell into a well, where he was stuck for hours. When his neighbors rescued him, he realized how the love of Jesus shone through their lives. After he was baptized, he wanted to share that love with others; so he went around pushing people down wells.

Sometimes we think that when it comes to the Christian experience, one size fits all.

What about your walk with Christ is unique? What part of your stories do you have in common with other people? Which experiences bring us together? Why does diversity of experience drive some people apart? When have you experienced diversity of experience in a good way? When have you experienced this in a difficult way?

Where do you find mystery and awe in worship? What brings God to life in a special and powerful way for you?

# 4.

# House Rules

*Ephesians 4–6*

## Claim Your Story

One bitter Chicago January while I was in seminary, we had the coldest and snowiest winter on record. Everyone had car trouble. We were poor as church mice, so we all drove old beaters that we parked outdoors. It was a constant trial. Every morning I would bundle up, go outside, dig out the car from a snow bank, and then try to start it so my wife could go to work.

That winter I was taking a class on Ephesians, and one student argued vigorously with the professor that the cosmic battle it describes had nothing to do with good works on earth. No matter. The proof is in the pudding. One morning I missed class trying to get the car started with no success, but that student also missed class because he was helping me. He said, "I can't go study Ephesians if my brother is in trouble." That's what Ephesians is all about: a cosmic battle between heaven and the spirits of the air—but with earthly implications. We all have a part to play.

What obstacles do you face spiritually?

What part have you played in the cosmic battle?

Have you ignored an opportunity for ministry?

Have you put church first over people?

## Enter the Bible Story

### *The Household of God*

When you play Monopoly at someone else's home, you have to establish the house rules—you know, the stuff that's not in the rulebook but everybody does, like putting all the fines from Chance and Community Chest in the middle and the first one just visiting jail gets to keep it.

The apostle Paul knew that they had household rules in Ephesus, that is to say, in the Roman households, which operated differently from Jewish society. Paul knew the household rules for Ephesus and spoke within that framework. That framework can be uncomfortable for us. If we read Ephesians 5:22–6:9 without understanding how those households worked, and especially without reading the verse that precedes 5:22 ("Submit to each other out of respect for Christ" [5:21].), we will come up with all kinds of funny ideas about the "biblical" family.

A civil rights worker once told me, "We can't always change attitudes, but we *can* regulate behavior." Thanks to the civil rights movement (based as it was in Christian nonviolence) and the legislation that grew out of it, a major transformation in race relations and human rights has evolved in our country. But for Paul the exact opposite was true.

The early Christians could not vote out the emperor of the Roman Empire and vote in a better one. Paul, therefore, could not regulate behavior; so he had to work on attitude. Since he could not change the structure of the Roman household, he worked to transform the way it operated. Paul worked with the Ephesians to create the Christian household of God.

I used to consider the household passage in the Letter to the Ephesians to be one part of the New Testament I would have ripped out if I could have. I was deeply troubled by its acceptance of slavery and its patriarchal model for marriage, as least as it is understood by some Christians, which is not only counterintuitive but also unworkable.

That was before I came to understand how the Roman household structure worked. First, all authority included accountability *and* responsibility. The Roman household was headed by a *paterfamilias*, who was an autocrat with the power of life or death over everyone. He arranged marriages, settled all disputes, and had physical and sexual control over everybody in the household. But he also had the responsibility of seeing to it that everyone was taken care of; and he provided the social safety net for the extended family, the slaves, the servants, the poets, artists, and all those involved in the household's business.

Paul insisted on an attitude change in the *paterfamilias*, demanding that if the husband is the head of the wife and thus of the whole family, he must act "like Christ [who] is head of the church, that is, the savior of the body" (Ephesians 5:23). Considering that Christ took on the form of a slave and washed the feet of his disciples, served others, and was obedient even to enduring death on a cross, we can see how the whole idea of headship had been transformed.

Anyone, therefore, who thinks Ephesians 5 means the husband is the undisputed master and everyone else has to do what the husband says doesn't understand the Scripture, or the Christianized Roman household, or marriage for that matter!

### *Communion Is Served*

The husband might be the head of the household, but someone had to run it. The administration of the Roman household was in the hands of the wife, who handled finances, ran the family, and provided daily leadership in the home.[1] The household had public areas where business took place, work areas for all those involved in the family business, and family areas for daily living. This is where the wife took charge in the Christianized Roman household. This included the church life, too. The preparation and administration of the Communion meal, or love feast, was the province of women. That's why early Christian Communion art shows women in charge.

Anyone who reads the New Testament realizes that women such as Mary the mother of Mark, Priscilla, Lydia, the apostle Junia, and others were leaders of the early church. I like what Carolyn Osiek and Margaret Y. MacDonald say in their book *A Woman's Place*: "To step into a Christian house church was to step into women's world."[2]

In addition to the women, who would have had responsibility for the management of the physical aspects of the household (including preparing and serving the aforementioned Communion meal), the household also included servants, slaves, relatives, artisans, and all those involved in the family's craft. In addition, there would have been, as Paul listed, apostles, prophets, evangelists, pastors, and teachers (see Ephesians 4:11). Some, like pastors and teachers, could have been part of the household; others, like the apostles, prophets, and evangelists, would have been temporary residents who passed through. This is confirmed by other Christian documents, including an early Christian manual known as the *Didache*.

I think some people picture Paul's letters arriving at the one building that served as a worship center for all the Christians in a city. Actually, however, the church at Ephesus—and the churches at Corinth, Philippi, Rome, and Colossae—probably consisted of many house churches meeting separately in the various households.

The most disquieting aspect of the Ephesians Scripture is the acceptance of slavery. Slavery was ugly in the ancient world, but it was a different situation than the slavery of the pre-Civil War American South. Slaves were not considered members of an inferior subrace destined for slavery. Slavery was a political or an economic condition. People became slaves because they were captured in war or because they could not keep up with their debts or because they were born into slavery. And since it was considered beneath the dignity of a free-born citizen to conduct business, slaves had great economic responsibility. Still, slavery was horrible.[3]

Christians had to create new households because the members of the ones they had belonged to worshiped the same god or gods together, gods that the new Christians could no longer honor. Becoming a Christian meant cutting economic as well as family ties. Creating the new household of God was therefore necessary for both salvation and economic survival.

### *Ready for Peace*

As Paul made clear to the Ephesians, they were engaged in a cosmic battle not "against human enemies but against rulers, authorities, forces of cosmic darkness, and spiritual powers of evil in the heavens" (6:12). In

Across the Testaments

### Order in the Court

*"Each of you must tell the truth to your neighbor"* (Ephesians 4:25) is taken from Zechariah 8:16. In the larger context of this passage, lying includes especially the false oaths that undermine the justice of the community. This is a direct rebellion against God. When the courts are no longer trustworthy, God's plan for a safe and sane society comes to nothing. This is consistent with the message of Ephesians, that our part of the cosmic battle includes justice, truth, and right behavior toward each other.

contrast to the *Pax Romana* (the "Peace of Rome"), which was based on the simple formula "Do what we say or we'll stomp you," the Peace of Christ involves submitting to each other in the name of Christ.

Such a battle requires armor, but what looks at first like militaristic imagery ends up being the language of peace. The armor in that battle is truth, justice, the good news of peace, faith, salvation, and God's Word. And our battle plan requires that we treat each other ethically!

We are to watch what comes out of our mouths. We are to be "kind, compassionate, and forgiving to each other" (Ephesians 4:32). Our good works are the direct response to God's grace! Power is best expressed in submission and service.

All this was demonstrated by the way God acted through Christ. This was in stark contrast to the behavior of the gods the Ephesians worshiped. These gods cavorted on the earth, impregnating women, cheating on each other, using humans as pawns, and in general leaving death and destruction in their wake. By contrast, Jesus is depicted (with reference to Psalm 68:18) as having descended "into the lower regions" before climbing "*to the heights*" to give gifts to the people (Ephesians 4:8-10). These gifts included drawing all the nations into the inheritance of God's people. This was accomplished through the cross.

About the Christian Faith

### Look Out Below

"What does the phrase 'he climbed up' mean if it doesn't mean that he had first gone down into the lower regions, the earth?" (Ephesians 4:9).

The mystery of Jesus going down into the lower regions (referenced indirectly in the phrase in the Apostles' Creed "he descended into hell") is something alluded to in more than one place in the New Testament. Over the centuries, Christians have interpreted this as the action of Jesus in that period between the Crucifixion and Resurrection during which Jesus set free the righteous who had lived before the salvation offered through the cross. I am reluctant to say more than Scripture says, except to observe that these texts seem to testify that God through Jesus has gone to extraordinary and even unimaginable lengths to bring us all together in one family.

Living the new life means transformation in all things, even anger. Some anger is good. When we think about relief supplies that don't make it to the starving because corrupt governments sell the supplies through the black market, when we think about the fact that slavery still exists in our world, when we consider what poor stewards we have been of the creation that God has put in our care, when we remember the blessed image of God that is to be found in every person, how can we fail to be angry? Jesus himself was angry when he saw what had happened to the Temple with the moneychangers and the merchants.

Yet Paul wrote, "*Be angry without sinning.* Don't let the sun set on your anger" (Ephesians 4:26). What is bad is holding on to anger. What we say and do matters, and everything should be for the building up of the community that is the creation of Christ.

Anger is only part of it, however. Paul gave the Ephesians a grim description of their old way of life, how in ignorance they lacked all sense of right and wrong, how some did whatever felt good rather than what was good for them (see Ephesians 4:17-19). It's a difficult balancing act.

At least some in the Christian community managed to live in the world while remaining separate from the Roman Empire. Sometime in the second century, an anonymous Christian composed a letter to an official named Diognetus defending believers as good citizens. He countered rumors that Christians participated in strange and unnatural practices. He asserted that followers of Christ might have been noncomformists, but they did their best to be good neighbors:

> For Christians don't come from other countries, speak a different language, or act differently. They don't have their own economies, or dialect, nor do they have bizarre lifestyles. . . . They live according to chance in both Greek speaking and foreign cities, and dress the same, eat the same foods, act the same in all the rest of life's ways—except that they also live paradoxically differently because of their citizenship. They live in the same countries, but they are foreigners. They take part in the political life of their land, but they endure the hardships of aliens. . . . They live on the earth but they are citizens of heaven. . . . They are put to death, but they are brought to life. They are made poor, but they make many rich. . . . People curse them but they bless in return. They honor those who insult them. . . . Simply put, Christians are to the world what the soul is to the body [author's translation].[4]

*Celebrate and Sing*

The patterns of worship described in Ephesians were similar to those of the synagogue: "Speak to each other with psalms, hymns, and spiritual songs; sing and make music to the Lord in your hearts; always give thanks to God the Father for everything" (Ephesians 5:19-20). Synagogue worship was different from Temple worship. One did not have to be a priest to lead worship in the synagogue. All were welcome to attend and take part. It seems from some passages as if anyone, including Gentiles, might attend. But in the Temple, only a chosen priesthood could perform the rites; and there were consecutive layers of exclusion—first of the Gentiles, then of the women, then of all men but the priests, then finally of all priests except the High Priest in the Holy of Holies.

Christian worship was more like synagogue worship than Temple worship. The difference was one of relationship. The relationship in the

Temple was hierarchical; the Christian faith involved a different kind of relationship with God. As Paul noted, "Marriage is a significant allegory, and I'm applying it to Christ and the church" (Ephesians 5:32). We are collectively the bride of Christ. We are in a holy embrace with God. We are called to be in a faithful and monogamous relationship with the One who made us.

That also means that it's time we grew up. We are no longer to be "tossed and blown around by every wind that comes from teaching with deceitful scheming and the tricks people play to deliberately mislead others" (Ephesians 4:14). The fads and deceits that come from inside as well as from outside the Christian church should no longer excite us. People are deceived when someone quotes a few Scripture verses out of context. Talking heads sound authoritative and confuse the truth. A spiritual fad sounds vaguely biblical, and sincere Christians wonder if such things are true.

This letter to the Ephesians calls upon us to grow up and grow into our new relationship with God and each other through Christ, submitting to and loving one another and building up the body. In some ways, things haven't changed over the years since Paul wrote this letter. The Ephesians were tempted with the mystery religions of magic and hierarchy. We are tempted with philosophies that suggest we control the universe through our minds. Deceits such as prosperity gospels, which suggest God wants us to be rich at the expense of the world's poor, abound. We allow ourselves to be comforted with the notion that all of our prejudices against ethnic groups, immigrants, outsiders, and the poor are appropriate because of what a few deceivers say, misquoting Scripture. We encourage the heresies that God favors a few (usually us and our friends) and does not desire the salvation of all. We allow the misinterpretation of Scripture to "uglify" the household of God so that it becomes a household of hierarchy, power, and domination. We encourage the delusions of those who believe they have solved the mystery, "cracked the code," and possess the knowledge that Jesus told us was denied even to him: the hour of his return (Matthew 24:36).

How much simpler to follow the advice of this passage of Scripture: "Imitate God like dearly loved children. Live your life with love, following

About the Scripture

### Boon Companion

Tychicus is identified at the end of this letter (Ephesians 6:21) as not only the bearer of the letter but also as an emissary with authority to describe the subtleties surrounding Paul's imprisonment. He was a Christian from Asia (Acts 20:4), a trusted emissary Paul sent to Colossae, Ephesus, and Crete who seems to have had some earlier connection to Ephesus (see Colossians 4:7; 2 Timothy 4:12; and Titus 3:12). Some commentators who question Paul's authorship of this letter have suggested that Tychicus was the actual writer of Ephesians.

the example of Christ, who loved us and gave himself for us" (Ephesians 5:1-2). Love, after all, is not a fad or a deceit. It is the way of Christ.

Living lives of service and submission to each other as one people demonstrates most clearly that we have been reconciled to God through Christ. The cross has that power.

## Live the Story

I'm part of our local jail chaplaincy. Prisoners often mention how much of their life has been wasted on foolish things and that when they are released, they will have to change their lives and their friends—to change households if you will—if they don't want to return to jail. Changes will have to be made.

I like the way the Common English Bible puts it: "Thieves should no longer steal. Instead they should go to work, using their hands to do good so that they will have something to share with whoever is in need" (Ephesians 4:28).

Well, it's easy to point out the changes that someone else needs to make. What about you and me? What part of our old life do we cling to? Do we cherish anger, letting the sun set on our passions?

Is there a sin you are almost proud of? Are you using your skills in a business or industry that harms more than it helps? Do you insist that someone will make or buy this product anyway, so it doesn't matter? Are you stealing your salvation from yourself?

In what ways have you wasted your time?

What myths define your life?

1. From *A Woman's Place*, by Carolyn Osiek and Margaret Y. MacDonald (Fortress Press, 2006); page 163.

2. From *A Woman's Place*, by Carolyn Osiek and Margaret Y. MacDonald; page 163.

3. From *Stewards, Prophets, Keepers of the Word*, by Ritva H. Williams (Hendrickson Publishers, 2006); pages 56–57.

4. See "The Epistle to Diognetus," in *The Apostolic Fathers*, translated by Kirsopp Lake (Harvard University Press, 1913, 1976); Volume II, page 361.

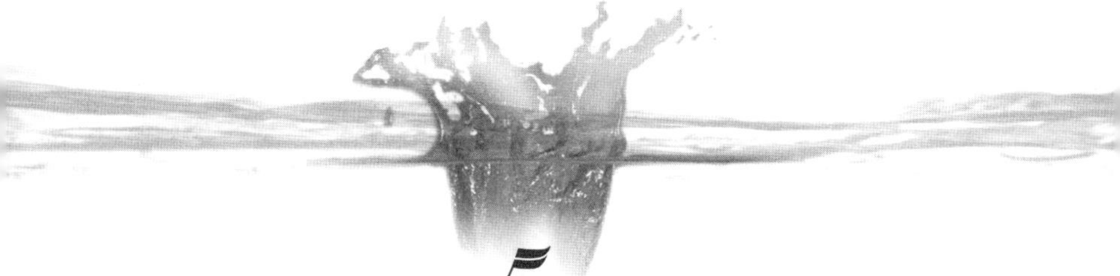

# 5.

# Unquenchable Joy

*Philippians 1–2*

## Claim Your Story

I grew up in a military family. We moved a lot. Maybe that's why I tend to think of home as the place where I happen to hang my hat at that particular moment. One thing I remember from those days is that we identified not with our current locale, but with something larger: the United States Navy. That identity gave meaning to our lives. It brought us joy.

Citizens of Philippi in Macedonia were also citizens of the Roman Empire. That larger identity gave meaning to their lives. Paul wanted the Christians in Philippi to know they were part of something even larger than Rome: They were citizens of heaven. Although they had not been reared with Bible stories, the Bible was now their story! And that brought them joy.

Name the levels of allegiance that you recognize. How do you prioritize those levels of authority?

Do you truly place Jesus first? Have you ever been willing to compromise your faith as a disciple of Jesus during times of fear, national crisis, or political fear mongering?

Is joy a regular part of your faith?

## Enter the Bible Story

### *A Prisoner for God*

In Hollywood they say that there's no such thing as bad publicity. Any publicity, good or bad, will benefit the movie, the star, the production company. Paul seems to have been saying something of the same sort when he wrote to the Philippians to tell them that his imprisonment, far from causing him shame, had "actually advanced the gospel. The whole Praetorian Guard and everyone else knows that I'm in prison for Christ" (Philippians 1:12-13).

Which imprisonment, when it took place, and how it ended is hard to determine from the letter. There are several theories, with suggestions that Paul wrote from Ephesus, Caesarea, or some unknown city. One of the more compelling theories is that the letter was written from Rome. Paul was kept under house arrest there for at least two years on one occasion, and he seems to have been imprisoned in much more dire circumstances a few years later. References to the Praetorian Guard (1:13) and Caesar's household (4:22) are also clues pointing to Rome. Like the Letter to the Ephesians, Philippians might have been written in A.D. 60 or in 64. Regardless of when or where he was imprisoned, Paul was facing a capital charge (see 1:20-21).

Philippi, a town of around 10,000 people in Macedonia, rested midway on the Via Egnatia, the Roman road that connected Asia Minor to the Adriatic. Although originally settled because of its gold reserves, a nonrenewable resource that had played out long ago, Philippi became better known for its agriculture.

Founded by Philip of Macedon in the fourth century B.C. (and named in his honor), it became a Roman colony after battles near Philippi in the year 42 B.C. led to victories by Antony and Octavius over Cassius and Brutus. This meant that for all intents and purposes, citizens of Philippi were living in Rome. They were granted the privileges, responsibilities, and tax benefits of Roman citizens.

Some of those who lived there had moved from Rome. Others were retired from Roman military service; and even though they had never seen Rome, they had served Rome throughout their careers. Their citizenship was their reward. Still others were born into their citizenship. All were proud of their Roman citizenship, language, and heritage.

Paul's initial missionary journey to Philippi came as the direct result of a revelation—a dream in which a man from Macedonia called to him for help (Acts 16:6-10). Oddly enough, although the call came from a man, the first convert in Macedonia turned out to be a woman: Lydia, a rich woman who had apparently been granted a monopoly to produce purple dye, used exclusively by royalty (16:13-15). She was identified as "a Gentile God-worshipper" (16:14), a Gentile attracted to the one God of the Hebrew Scriptures. At least one of the Philippian house churches was associated with her household, which probably included extended family, servants, slaves, artisans, and others supported by her business.

Normally, Paul would have met first with the men who gathered in a town's synagogue, which tended to be his initial stop in a new city. There is little archaeological evidence of a Jewish presence in Philippi, however. Without ten men, there was no quorum for Jewish worship. As a result, when Paul arrived, he looked for believers at the riverside, where he found a group of women, including Lydia, who prayed together (Acts 16:13).

The Philippian church was indeed an eclectic group. Women, including Euodia and Syntyche (See the next chapter in this study.) and, of course, Lydia, seem to have been heavily involved in the church's leadership. Another early convert was the man who had been Paul's jailer (see Acts 16:25-34); he would have belonged to one of the house churches, along with the others alluded to in the letter.

Paul's exciting ministry in Philippi ended after his cure of a slave girl possessed by an evil spirit destroyed her financial value to her owners. After his arrest on trumped-up charges, his false imprisonment (Acts 16:16-24), and his eventual release (16:35-40), the apostle stayed in touch with the church.

### *The Commonwealth of Christ*

Even though the Letter to the Philippians was written from the equivalent of a modern-day death row, the theme is joy. There is joy to be found in Jesus, who himself set the example by willingly embracing shame and being elevated by God.

Like many congregations, ancient and modern, the Philippians faced the sort of problems that arise because there are people in the church. We're only human, so sometimes we don't get along. But Paul's prayer was that their love would grow and that they would "be able to decide what really matters" (Philippians 1:10).

In this letter, Paul did not refer to Abraham, Sarah, Moses, or the prophets because he was writing to people who did not grow up with the Hebrew Bible. He used another line of reasoning, one they would understand because as Philippians they were also Romans. They experienced the joys, the privileges, and the responsibilities of being Roman citizens. Paul insisted that they were also citizens of a place they had never seen: heaven.

Paul says this clearly in Philippians 3:20 (which will be discussed in the next chapter); but it is also implicit when he says, "Live together in a manner worthy of Christ's gospel" (1:27). The verb involved in this verse, *politeuomai*, might also be translated as "living politically," or "living responsibly," or "living as mutually accountable citizens."

I live in one of the states that describe themselves as commonwealths. In a practical sense, that may not make much difference politically; but I love the idea that as citizens of a free state we not only have rights but also the responsibility to share the wealth in common for the benefit of all.

The apostle was calling on the Philippians to conduct themselves as citizens, as "commonwealthers," of Christ's gospel. The word *politeuomai* comes from the idea of the Greek city-state, where all were connected and all were accountable to each other.

As citizens of the gospel, citizens of heaven, each problem in the church is our problem. We have a stake in each other's woes. Being a citizen of the body of Christ is more than just saying we're saved; it is living in fellowship and community with each other.

If the Philippians could act as a commonwealth, their problems would be solved. Their enemies would be powerless against them. They would be able to face persecution and distress together. If they did so, Paul wrote, they would "complete my joy by thinking the same way, having the same love, being united, and agreeing with each other" (Philippians 2:2).

What does that mean? What does it mean to "stand firm, united in one spirit and mind" (Philippians 1:27)? Does it mean we have to share the same politics? Must we listen to the same music? Are we in the same economic bracket? Were those who pestered the Galatians to drop their ethnic identity and become like them (see Chapter 1 of this study) correct after all?

*They're Playing Our Song*

It depends on what we intend to stand firm for. And that is made absolutely clear in what is known as the Christ hymn (Philippians 2:5-11). We are to stand united in imitating Jesus as servants—no, as *slaves*—to each other, emptying ourselves that we may be filled with Christ, to the end that the whole of creation may acknowledge Jesus as Lord.

We do not know whether Paul wrote the Christ hymn or was quoting it, but it doesn't really matter. By placing it in this letter, it has become his song.

Songs are powerful, in part because music uses a different portion of our brain. It cuts to the heart of the matter. I remember hearing a radio interview of a former POW from the Vietnamese War talk about how important Scriptures were in keeping up his spirits and those of his fellow prisoners. He recalled how they would tap them out in code along the pipes connecting their cells. When someone asked the former POW to recite these Scriptures, it turned out they were not Bible verses but hymns. The hymns were the best expressions of their faith.

The Christ hymn itself, like the rest of this letter, was written in Greek; but the hymn does not work as Greek poetry. Its rhythms and its use of parallel images seem more like Hebrew poetry. I suspect Paul wrote this hymn in another language and translated it into the Greek. But that doesn't matter. What matters is what the hymn says, especially when it is compared with what the competition was claiming.

The Roman emperor was considered to be a god and a descendant of a god. Since Rome had conquered the Western world and eliminated the petty wars that constantly raged between kings of small kingdoms, there were those who considered the emperor to be the prince of peace and the savior of the world. The equivalent of a god, the Roman emperor expected abject obedience, lived in luxury, and lorded it over all.

David R. Wallace, in his book *The Gospel of God: Romans as Paul's Aeneid*, suggests that Virgil wrote his classic poem the *Aeneid* to demonstrate that Homer's epics, the *Iliad* and the *Odyssey*, were considered scriptures of a sort in the ancient world. Virgil's *Aeneid* was meant to prophesy the emergence of Augustus Caesar as the ruler foretold by the ancient writings, the prince of peace, the savior of the world, a god and the descendant of gods, the lord of lords.[1] Christians believed someone else filled that description a lot better. In his letters, Paul proclaimed something we know to be the truth: Jesus, not Caesar, was the fulfillment of the ancient writings and filled the bill in all these particulars.

The Christian message that Jesus "was in the form of God" (Philippians 2:6) made sense to the Philippians. They now knew who the real prince of peace and savior of the world was. They now proclaimed—the height of treason—that Jesus was Lord, not that Caesar was Lord. Through this hymn Paul reminded them that Jesus, unlike the emperor, "did not consider being equal with God something to exploit" for luxurious living and worldly power (Philippians 2:6). The story of Jesus resisting temptation in the wilderness made that clear (Matthew 4:1-11).

Like the sort of drink offering the Philippians would have been familiar with, poured out sizzling over the hot altar, Jesus emptied himself and took the form not of an emperor, but of a slave (see Philippians 2:17). This humility of obedience, which Paul claimed would help the Philippians achieve one mind in Christ, stretched even to the point of submitting to the cross.

Because we wear the cross on jewelry and it is an ever-present symbol in our society, we have lost touch with what the Philippians knew intimately: The cross was something so obscene, so horrifying, it was reserved for the dregs of society, the lowest of the low.

Crucifixion was meant to eradicate identity. Nothing was retained by the victims, not their name, not their clothes, not even their bodies, which were usually dumped in pits to be eaten by animals. But for Jesus, what was the result of this humiliation? In contrast to the emperor, whose name was honored only within the confines of the empire, at the name of Jesus everyone, everywhere in the cosmos, "in heaven, on earth, and under

About the Scripture

## Straw Bosses and Waiters

The word *episkopoi* is sometimes translated "bishops," but the CEB is literally correct when it renders the word as "supervisors" or "overseers" in the greeting of Paul's letter to the Philippians (1:1). The word referred to a slave or servant who was appointed by the master to supervise the work in the fields or the factory, a straw boss. The overseer in the early Christian community was as much concerned with the financial and economic well-being of the community as with the spiritual maintenance. It was not just an ecclesiastical office. Another word commonly mistranslated, *diakonoi*, means "table waiter" more than our conception of "deacon." One of their chief functions was ensuring that all were fed and cared for at the common table.

the earth" (Philippians 2:10), would bow and confess the ultimate treason: "Jesus Christ is Lord" (2:11).

This humiliation of donning the guise of a slave and humbling oneself in obedience and service was exemplified in the shocking actions of Jesus, who girded himself with a towel and like a slave washed the feet of his disciples at the Last Supper (John 13:1-9). That the first Christians performed this same act in imitation of Jesus is well attested in early church literature. Some commentators interpret the Christ hymn as symbolizing the act of foot washing, and this hymn was perhaps even sung during the ritual.

This service both as fellow slaves and members of the same cosmic commonwealth was personified in Epaphroditus, whom the Philippians sent to serve Paul in prison. They continued to take care of Paul because they were one commonwealth. Paul sent Epaphroditus back to the Philippians after Epaphroditus barely survived an illness. Each had the welfare of the other in mind (Philippians 2:25-30).

The strength of that commonwealth is further demonstrated by Paul's statement that has sometimes been suggested as being suicidal: "Because for me, living serves Christ and dying is even better" (Philippians 1:21). Paul was not at all depressed, however. He believed that dying would bring

About the Christian Faith

## Model Prisoner

In 1714, Wilhelm Grahe was arrested in Solingen, Germany, along with several other religious separatists. They were accused of the crimes of being baptized by immersion as an adult, taking part in home Bible studies, and refusing to be a part of the established state church. They were taken to Dusseldorf; and on February 26, 1717, Grahe, along with five others, was found guilty of treason and heresy. They were sentenced to imprisonment in the fortress at Julich to serve what was meant to be a fatal term at hard labor.[2]

On the way to Julich, Grahe fell two thousand yards behind the others. A bystander asked why he didn't escape. He replied that guards were not necessary "because Jesus, His truth and teaching were our protection and solace."[3]

Grahe worked at a backbreaking pace all day while imprisoned. Nights were spent in cold, lice-ridden, dank cells in all weathers alongside dangerous criminals.

After almost four years, Grahe was released along with his companions. They were all so weak that they could not walk but were returned home by cart. Their survival was seen as a triumphant vindication of their faithfulness.

reward; and since he had suffered greatly already and was facing possible death, he was being realistic. If he died, it wouldn't be because he chose to take his life but because the Roman authorities recognized his allegiance to Jesus as a threat to imperial authority.

Because Paul and the Philippians were part of the same commonwealth, he wrote, "It's more important for me to stay in this world for your sake" (Philippians 1:24). The Philippians' needs were more important to him than his immediate reward. Being slaves to each other meant joy and more joy.

So now that we know how to solve the problem the Philippians were facing, what exactly caused Paul to write this letter? What was the threat to their joy? The problem was not theological, or cultural, or one of practice, that is to say, how do we conduct baptism, Communion, or anointing. It was much more complicated.

The problem, which will be discussed more fully in the next chapter, was simple: A couple of the women of the church were fighting about leadership.

## Live the Story

For a few Christian groups, acting "politically" as part of the commonwealth of God as Paul suggested when he wrote, "Live together in a manner worth of Christ's gospel" (Philippians 1:27) meant pooling everyone's funds in one purse, living in the same building, and having all possessions in common. Although some Christians, such as the Hutterites, have made a successful go of such an arrangement, most, like the followers of Conrad Beissel at the Ephrata Cloisters in colonial Pennsylvania, have not lasted that long. This way of life doesn't seem to work in the real world.

The Philippians had a lot to unlearn as well as learn. They had inherited the Greek belief in a dim and shadowy afterlife in Hades, where most people were neither rewarded nor punished but simply longed for the bright light of the outer world. This belief injected a melancholy sadness that infected even the happy moments of life.

The Philippians' new faith in Christ required them to turn this worldview upside down. Because of the resurrection of Jesus Christ, they too had the resurrection of the dead to look forward to—and a glorious life to come that would overshadow everything they had experienced in the present world. This is why the word *joy* permeates every aspect of the Letter to the Philippians. Paul expected that this new outlook would, regardless of their circumstances, make joy the default setting for their lives, now lived in Christ.

What do you and your fellow church members do as "commonwealthers"? Do you collect money to benefit members of the church in case of emergency? If so, how is the fund administered?

How do you discreetly discover who needs help and channel it to them? How do you accomplish such aims without embarrassing others? (Whatever you do, don't say, "We're always ready to help someone who asks." Guess what? Most of them won't ask.)

Read Philippians 2:1-4 aloud. What does it mean to you to think alike, share the same love, remain united, and agree with each other? In your experience, have encouragement, comforting, sharing, and sympathizing completed the joy of your congregation? Where and when are you aware of the joy of Christ in your daily life?

1. From *The Gospel of God: Romans as Paul's Aeneid*, by David R. Wallace (Pickwick Publications, 2008); pages xvii, 39, 196–197.

2 From *The Brethren Encyclopedia* (The Brethren Encyclopedia, Inc., 1983); Volume 2, page 1201.

3. From *European Origins of the Brethren*, compiled and translated by Donald F. Durnbaugh (The Brethren Press, 1958); page 252.

# 6.

# The Heart of Joy

*Philippians 3–4*

## Claim Your Story

In my thirty years of experience as a pastor, moderator, and participant in the ecumenical community, I've been astounded that only rarely is conflict in churches about doctrine. No one argues about the virgin birth. One doesn't hear of a congregation splitting over the divinity of Jesus. No. People are angry about boilers, church kitchens, and the color of the sanctuary. I remember one congregation that was bitterly divided over which brand of vitamins was most Christlike. In another church, a pro-toilet group installed a commode in the middle of the night without permission from the church board. The anti-toilet group plugged it with cement.

Although Paul tackled major theological issues in Philippians, in the final chapter he got down to the real problem: There were two church women who didn't get along. What was the conflict about? The letter doesn't tell us, but no doubt it would have looked small to an outsider but felt like life or death to the participants.

What has been the most difficult problem you've ever faced in your church? What was it about? Do you even want to bring it up for fear of the conflict bursting into flame again?

We are on the road to glory. What roadblocks stand in the way?

## Enter the Bible Story

*The Finish Line*

I decided to run my first marathon when I was in my thirties—after losing sixty pounds and working hard to get back into shape. I'm really not athletic, and I'm certainly not fast; but my spiritual upbringing taught me to endure. Slowly I built my physical endurance, always reminding myself whenever it got hard how important achieving this goal was to me.

During the actual race, I was surprised when, at mile 16, I developed what I can only call chemical depression. All the inspiration was gone, all the joy; only duty caused me to put one foot in front of the other. I put aside every distraction and kept running despite the fact that I didn't care anymore. But the emotional clouds cleared at mile 20; so even though the pain got worse, it was no trouble to continue. After I stumbled across the finish line after 26 miles, 385 yards, I began to weep with joy. Four hours, 12 minutes, and 6 seconds—no world record to be sure; but I had kept my eyes on the prize, and no one could take it from me.

Paul used the imagery of athletic competition to encourage the Philippians to endure because he knew that they were quite familiar with the agony of training and the joy of victory. The finish line in the ancient games was a flag. No matter how terrible the runners felt, all distractions were put aside as they focused on that pennant. In the same way, Paul wrote that although he hadn't yet reached the goal, he forgot every distraction and put one foot in front of the other, pursuing "the prize of God's upward call in Christ Jesus" (Philippians 3:14).

Paul was striving "that [he] may perhaps reach the goal of the resurrection of the dead" (Philippians 3:11). The Philippians, too, must bear in mind that their current trials would end in joy. They were not to lose sight of the ultimate goal even when they reached a place where only obedience would force them to put one foot in front of the other.

There may have been those who wanted them to stop training. Others might try to get them to slow down. But these "enemies of the cross" would end in destruction (Philippians 3:18-19).

John Chrysostom (ca. A.D. 347–407) preached about this whole idea of training and reward when he commented on how important it was to train for the eternal prize in a sermon on Philippians. He asked his hearers to see "the runners, how they live by rule, how they touch nothing that relaxes their strength, how they exercise themselves every day in the palæstra, under a master, and by rule. Imitate them, or rather exhibit even greater eagerness, for the prizes are not equal."[1]

Sports is all about stats. In the ancient world, monuments were erected to commemorate athletes and their statistics. In our time, statistics are everywhere: in newspapers, on the Internet, on the television screen, and on baseball cards. When I was a boy, I collected baseball cards. This was in the era before they were preserved in plastic cases as an investment. Mine were stacked together, with a rubber band around the middle; and all the doubles were clothes-pinned on the wheels of my bike to make what I imagined was the noise of a motorcycle.

I loved turning over the cards to read the statistics. These facts defined the player. Paul has shared his baseball cards with us, showing that if anyone has cause to boast in Christ, his stats outshine theirs!

### *Not Worth Spit*

The Philippian house churches were facing two great distractions, one from within and one from without. The outside distraction was caused by Christian believers who (as was the case in Galatia) wanted the Gentile believers to adopt Jewish practices. Remember that there was nothing intrinsically wrong with these practices. Paul observed them faithfully and received great benefit from them. But they were not mandatory.

Sometimes we think the church traditions we grew up with were not only great fun but are required of everyone. When I pastored in Los Angeles, folks hung around for an hour or more after worship, talking, laughing, sharing. People eat at all hours in LA, so no one had to rush off anywhere.

When I became a pastor in Indiana, I was shocked that the church emptied out immediately after worship. The parking lot was empty within ten minutes. I'd never experienced the tradition of the big Sunday dinner. Neither the Angelinos nor the Hoosiers are wrong. Both ways of life work just fine. These are local customs, not universal or even biblical, although you'd think when talking to some folks that it's not the Lord's Day without pot roast.

Certain Jewish Christians had been lording it over the Philippians because they thought they were the "real" believers. They did everything right—according to them. Paul responded by giving his stats: circumcised on the eighth day, an Israelite from the tribe of Benjamin (that good old genealogy name game), "a Hebrew of the Hebrews" (Philippians 3:5).

If that weren't enough, Paul was one of the good guys, a Pharisee. Although the Pharisees who appear in the New Testament give that branch of Judaism a bad name, they were generally the Jewish group most concerned with the plight of the ordinary people. They served the synagogues. They interpreted the law. Paul was not only a Pharisee, he had worked to keep the faith pure by persecuting Christians. No one could outdo him in what he had imagined was piety!

Yet all these statistics he considered "sewer trash" (Philippians 3:8) when compared to the joy of God's destiny for all. This was why he wanted the Philippians to put aside every distraction.

What Paul formerly called satisfaction had been replaced by "the righteousness that...comes from knowing Christ, the power of his resurrection, and the participation in his sufferings" (Philippians 3:10). His finish line now was "the goal of the resurrection of the dead" (3:11).

About the Scripture

## Rated PG

When Paul "wrote...off" his past accomplishments as "a loss" compared to knowing Christ (Philippians 3:7), he used a spectacularly vulgar term that the CEB translators delicately refer to as "sewer trash" (3:8). Paul's use of the "S-word" is a reminder that there is a difference between vulgarity and profanity. An observant Jew, Paul would have considered profanity the profaning of the name of God. He would never have used the name of God as casually as do many people who would never dream of letting a vulgar word escape their lips. But he used a vulgarity because it made a startling point in a startling fashion.

It helps to remember the Greco-Roman view of the afterlife as perceived in the ancient world and exemplified in epic poems like the *Odyssey* and the *Aeneid*, both of which many people considered scripture. The Greeks and Romans celebrated life frantically, and sometimes at the expense of others, because there was no joy hereafter. Hades was a grey place, indistinct, where the dead envied the living and longed for the bright sunshine of the upper world. A few might be singled out for reward—or more likely, punishment—in the next world; but otherwise, whether you lived well or poorly, your fate was the same. You were a shadow.

The Greeks and Romans were not alone in this. One Jewish group, known as the Sadducees, did not believe in the resurrection of the dead or any sort of afterlife.

The prospect of being raised with Christ caused Paul to tell the Philippians who had grown up with the myth of bleakness to "be glad in the Lord always! Again I say, be glad!" (Philippians 4:4). He asked them to complete his joy. This joy, to be experienced fully in heaven, is lived now despite all persecution and perils. Happiness, after all, is something we can create by doing the things we enjoy; but like a shallow stream, happiness can quickly dry up. Joy is like a deep underground pool whose depths have not been plumbed. Joy is the gift of God and endures despite pain and suffering.

### *One Step After Another*

To focus on what is not essential is to lose sight of the goal of the resurrection of the dead—which brings us to the second major problem in Philippi, the second distraction: Two women were not getting along.

If Paul was imprisoned in Rome at this time, it would probably have taken two months for word to get to him that Euodia and Syntyche were fighting (Philippians 4:2). It might have taken at least another two months for his letter to get back to the Philippians, begging them to get along. But time was not a factor. If you're a member of a church, you know that a good grudge in the name of Christ can go on for years.

Why?

The smallest things get blown out of proportion, and suddenly nothing is more important than the argument. All that matters to the antagonists, regardless of what happens to the church, is winning.

Maybe one reason a good church grudge can seem so important can be found in the ancient Olympic Games. In those days there was no second place. Almost all of those who sacrificed years of their lives in harsh training saw it go to waste when they finished out of first. The words of the popular bumper sticker "Second Place Is First Loser" would have made sense in the ancient Olympics. Perhaps Euodia and Syntyche assumed there was no room for compromise in a world without second place.

In God's plan for humankind, everyone can win. Christianity is not a reality show where contestants are eliminated one by one and only the craftiest, most manipulating, or most conniving Christian can inherit eternal life. All have a share of the reward. Both Euodia and Syntyche could be winners if they would reconcile with each other and with the church.

And it mattered. A whole church can go down the tubes when a fight like that takes over.

We do not know what the fight was about. But we do know that Paul wanted Syzygus (translated "loyal friend" in the CEB), Clement, and everyone else in the church to get involved (Philippians 4:3). Everyone in the church would have known about Paul's request because 2,000 years ago, there was no such thing as silent reading. All reading was done out loud; and for most people, reading meant listening to the person who could decipher the text. The letter would have been read aloud in the presence of everyone in the congregation—including Euodia and Syntyche.

Everyone in the commonwealth of believers has a stake in the health of the community. That means everyone is a potential arbiter. There's a fragment of a situation comedy written by the playwright Menander (342–291 B.C.) called *The Arbiters*. (Paul actually quoted Menander's play *Thais* in 1 Corinthians 15:33 when he wrote, "Bad company corrupts good character."[2]) In *The Arbiters*, two slaves, arguing over who owns found jewelry, stop a passing citizen and appeal to him to arbitrate their disagreement. At first, the citizen refuses; so they remind him that everyone has a stake in seeing justice done. The citizen agrees to listen to their arguments and settle their dispute.[3]

We also have a stake in church disputes. It's tempting to turn away and hope someone else will handle it or that it will all simply go away. But we are fellow members of the commonwealth of God.

The free citizens of Philippi, citizens of the Roman Empire because of their city's exalted state, would have taken great pride in their name being written down in the city's register. In his appeal to the believers to take time to work out their salvation together, Paul reminded them that their names were already registered in an even more important book: "the scroll of life" (Philippians 4:3).

Even in these circumstances of trouble, Paul insisted that they be glad. "The Lord is near" (Philippians 4:5). Both senses of the word *near* are meant here. That is, the Lord is literally near, always at hand, an unseen presence, a welcome auditor of all we say and do. So act like Jesus is with us because he is! The use of the word *near* also means that Jesus is coming again and has almost arrived; and when he does, he will be fully revealed. At the very least, that ought to affect the way we treat each other. The Philippians—and we too—are meant to live as people who are expecting something wonderful to happen at any moment! That's why it's possible for "the peace of God that exceeds all understanding" to keep our "hearts and minds safe in Christ Jesus" (4:7).

Having chided, Paul quickly returned to praise. In thanking the Philippians for sending Epaphroditus, he was also thanking them for their financial and physical support. It was one more way his misfortune was fortunate; his imprisonment had given them one more opportunity to demonstrate their mutual love.

Of course, we are the inheritors of the ministry of Paul today; so his letter is also to us. With all that is at stake, it's important that we be imitators of saints like Paul and watch all who live this way. We're not there yet.

The aforementioned Chrysostom got the same message from this letter to Philippi. He wrote, "He then, who thinks that all is accomplished, and that nothing is wanting to him for the perfecting of virtue,

About the Christian Faith

## In Care of the Birmingham Jail

Paul wasn't the only Christian unjustly imprisoned who wrote letters. Among the many who fit in this category was Dr. Martin Luther King, Jr., who in his famous "Letter From a Birmingham Jail" noted that he, like Paul must answer the Macedonian call for help. His challenge to his fellow Christians not to allow themselves to be distracted from God's justice included the admonition to repent not only for the poor behavior of the bad but also for the silence of the good.

may cease running, as having apprehended all. But he who thinks that he is still distant from the goal, will never cease running. This then we should always consider, even though we have wrought ten thousand good deeds."[4]

So keep running like you're almost there but not quite. That's the way to resurrection. That's the way to joy.

About the Scripture

## Generosity to Others

I know a pastor who sent his youth group out on a door-to-door can drive to stock a local food pantry. They did not go to the wealthiest neighborhood. In fact, most of those who donated had probably visited the food pantry themselves at one time or another. The folks were extremely generous. Those youth could hardly carry the haul!

Wildly enthused about their good fortune, the youth then proceeded to a nearby gated community. It was tough to gain entry and turned out to be a waste of time. They came away with almost nothing. It just goes to show that it's not what you have; it's what you give!

In his second letter to the Corinthians, Paul praised the Macedonians, which included the Philippians, for being so generous to the Jerusalem poor even though they themselves were impoverished (2 Corinthians 8:1-2). Now he thanked the Philippians for supporting his ministry when no one else did—even when he was off in Thessalonica—and it did not directly benefit them (Philippians 4:15-16).

## Live the Story

I met a wonderful man whose attitude was to accept tragedy as well as triumph, always reminding himself where his life's journey was headed. He shrugged off squabbles and controversies as unimportant compared to the goal of his life's journey: resurrection in Christ Jesus.

This man's strongest demonstration of belief came when his wife suffered a massive heart attack. When it became clear there was no hope for any real recovery, he asked that no drastic measures be used to extend her life. Her death saddened him, but it was not the end. He attended church faithfully until a few years later when the doctor told him he would die soon unless he began a series of painful treatments that might not work. He refused them. Death was not the journey's end, just the beginning.

Paul would have agreed. He told the Philippians the sufferings he endured were so that he might "reach the goal of the resurrection of the dead" (3:11). The Philippians were abandoning the myth of Hades for the daring promise of resurrection. Paul, like my friend, set an example by the way he lived and died.

How does your faith in the resurrection define your life's story? How does it affect your view of death?

What do you consider the "prize of God's upward call in Christ Jesus" (Philippians 3:14)? How do you share in it now?

Faith is action. "Our citizenship is in heaven" (Philippians 3:20). What will you do to make that obvious to the rest of the world?

1. From "Saint Chrysostom," in *Nicene and Post-Nicene Fathers of the Christian Church*, edited by Philip Schaff (Wm. B. Eerdmans Publishing Company, 1979); Volume XIII, page 239.

2. From *Menander*, translated by Francis G. Allinson (Harvard University Press, 1964); page 357.

3. From *Menander*, edited and translated by W.G. Arnott (Harvard University Press, 1979); pages 407–411.

4. From "Saint Chrysostom," in *Nicene and Post-Nicene Fathers of the Christian Church*, edited by Philip Schaff; Volume XIII, page 239.

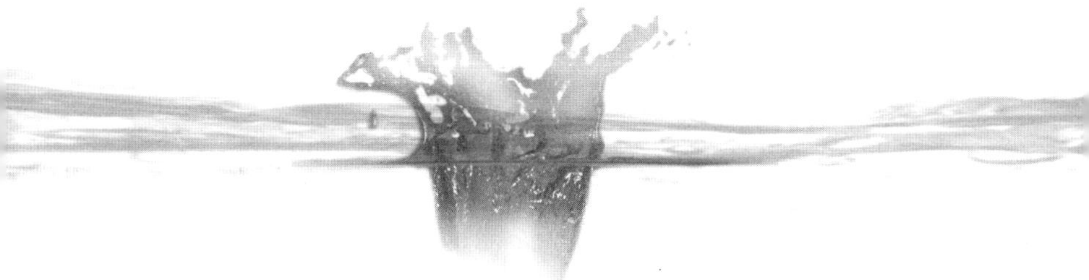

# Leader Guide

People often view the Bible as a maze of obscure people, places, and events from centuries ago and struggle to relate it to their daily lives. IMMERSION invites us to experience the Bible as a record of God's loving revelation to humankind. These studies recognize our emotional, spiritual, and intellectual needs and welcome us into the Bible story and into deeper faith.

As leader of an IMMERSION group, you will help participants to encounter the Word of God and the God of the Word that will lead to new creation in Christ. You do not have to be an expert to lead; in fact, you will participate with your group in listening to and applying God's life-transforming Word to your lives. You and your group will explore the building blocks of the Christian faith through key stories, people, ideas, and teachings in every book of the Bible. You will also explore the bridges and points of connection between the Old and New Testaments.

**Choosing and Using the Bible**

The central goal of IMMERSION is engaging the members of your group with the Bible in a way that informs their minds, forms their hearts, and transforms the way they live out their Christian faith. Participants will need this study book and a Bible. IMMERSION is an excellent accompaniment to the Common English Bible (CEB). It shares with the CEB four common aims: clarity of language, faith in the Bible's power to transform lives, the emotional expectation that people will find the love of God, and the rational expectation that people will find the knowledge of God.

Other recommended study Bibles include *The New Interpreter's Study Bible* (NRSV), *The New Oxford Annotated Study Bible* (NRSV), *The HarperCollins Study Bible* (NRSV), *the NIV and TNIV Study Bibles*, and the

*Archaeological Study Bible* (NIV). Encourage participants to use more than one translation. *The Message: The Bible in Contemporary Language* is a modern paraphrase of the Bible, based on the original languages. Eugene H. Peterson has created a masterful presentation of the Scripture text, which is best used alongside rather than in place of the CEB or another primary English translation.

One of the most reliable interpreters of the Bible's meaning is the Bible itself. Invite participants first of all to allow Scripture to have its say. Pay attention to context. Ask questions of the text. Read every passage with curiosity, always seeking to answer the basic Who? What? Where? When? and Why? questions.

Bible study groups should also have handy essential reference resources in case someone wants more information or needs clarification on specific words, terms, concepts, places, or people mentioned in the Bible. A Bible dictionary, Bible atlas, concordance, and one-volume Bible commentary together make for a good, basic reference library.

**The Leader's Role**

An effective leader prepares ahead. This leader guide provides easy to follow, step-by-step suggestions for leading a group. The key task of the leader is to guide discussion and activities that will engage heart and head and will invite faith development. Discussion questions are included, and you may want to add questions posed by you or your group. Here are suggestions for helping your group engage Scripture:

State questions clearly and simply.

Ask questions that move Bible truths from "outside" (dealing with concepts, ideas, or information about a passage) to "inside" (relating to the experiences, hopes, and dreams of the participants).

Work for variety in your questions, including compare and contrast, information recall, motivation, connections, speculation, and evaluation.

Avoid questions that call for yes-or-no responses or answers that are obvious.

Don't be afraid of silence during a discussion. It often yields especially thoughtful comments.

Test questions before using them by attempting to answer them yourself.

When leading a discussion, pay attention to the mood of your group by "listening" with your eyes as well as your ears.

## Guidelines for the Group

IMMERSION is designed to promote full engagement with the Bible for the purpose of growing faith and building up Christian community. While much can be gained from individual reading, a group Bible study offers an ideal setting in which to achieve these aims. Encourage participants to bring their Bibles and read from Scripture during the session. Invite participants to consider the following guidelines as they participate in the group:

Respect differences of interpretation and understanding.

Support one another with Christian kindness, compassion, and courtesy.

Listen to others with the goal of understanding rather than agreeing or disagreeing.

Celebrate the opportunity to grow in faith through Bible study.

Approach the Bible as a dialogue partner, open to the possibility of being challenged or changed by God's Word.

Recognize that each person brings unique and valuable life experiences to the group and is an important part of the community.

Reflect theologically—that is, be attentive to three basic questions: What does this say about God? What does this say about me/us? What does this say about the relationship between God and me/us?

Commit to a *lived faith response* in light of insights you gain from the Bible. In other words, what changes in attitudes (how you believe) or actions (how you behave) are called for by God's Word?

**Group Sessions**

The group sessions, like the chapters themselves, are built around three sections: "Claim Your Story," "Enter the Bible Story," and "Live the Story." Sessions are designed to move participants from an awareness of their own life story, issues, needs, and experiences into an encounter and dialogue with the story of Scripture and to make decisions integrating their personal stories and the Bible's story.

The session plans in the following pages will provide questions and activities to help your group focus on the particular content of each chapter. In addition to questions and activities, the plans will include chapter title, Scripture, and faith focus.

Here are things to keep in mind for all the sessions:

*Prepare Ahead*

Study the Scripture, comparing different translations and perhaps a paraphrase.

Read the chapter, and consider what it says about your life and the Scripture.

Gather materials such as large sheets of paper or a markerboard with markers.

Prepare the learning area. Write the faith focus for all to see.

*Welcome Participants*

Invite participants to greet one another.

Tell them to find one or two people and talk about the faith focus.

Ask: What words stand out for you? Why?

*Guide the Session*

Look together at "Claim Your Story." Ask participants to give their reactions to the stories and examples given in each chapter. Use questions from the session plan to elicit comments based on personal experiences and insights.

Ask participants to open their Bibles and "Enter the Bible Story." For each portion of Scripture, use questions from the session plan to help participants gain insight into the text and relate it to issues in their lives.

Step through the activity or questions posed in "Live the Story." Encourage participants to embrace what they have learned and apply it in their daily lives.

Invite participants to offer their responses or insights about the boxed material in "Across the Testaments," "About the Scripture," and "About the Christian Faith."

*Close the Session*

Encourage participants to read the following week's Scripture and chapter before the next session.

Offer a closing prayer.

# 1. We Are What We Are

*Galatians 1:1–5:12*

## Faith Focus

Although the law is of great benefit to teach us the way of God, it is through faith in Jesus Christ that we become right with God.

## Before the Session

Read Chapter 1 in the study and the assigned chapters and verses from Galatians. In magazines or on the Internet, find some pictures of families from different cultures eating different foods. Take these pictures to the session to display to "prime the pump" for the discussion of cultural differences.

## Claim Your Story

Invite participants to share their stories about when they first realized that everyone was not just like them. Suggest that they tell what their reaction was. Ask participants: When you discovered that other families did things differently from how your family did them or other church groups worshiped differently from how your church group worshiped, were you confused? interested? judgmental? excited? frightened? had some other feeling?

Next, invite participants to tell how those initial feelings changed as they gained a wider experience of the world. Ask: How do your understandings of the range of human differences fit with your understanding of what people must have in common to be followers of Jesus? What are the implications of the comment in the study that "we're one in Christ and different in everything else" (page 9)?

Then ask the group to consider these questions: What assumptions do you make about what is "normal"? When it comes to our Christian faith, what is essential?

## Enter the Bible Story

### Beginnings

Ask group members, from their reading of the "Beginnings" section of the study, to name some ways in which the culture and the political circumstances of the first century were very different from ours. In terms of culture, participants might mention the matter of women not eating with men, Jews not eating with Greeks, slaves not eating with free. In terms of politics, they might mention people with little in common being forced together into regions of the Roman Empire.

Then ask in what ways are there similarities between the first-century culture and our own. One similarity might be our tendency to spend the majority of our time with people who are similar to us. What are the benefits of that in terms of living our faith in Jesus? What are the drawbacks of that in terms of living our faith?

Many group members will likely be surprised to learn that Galatians were Celts. Ask them to list, again from their reading of the "Beginnings" section of the study, the general characteristics of Celts. Then invite participants to imagine they are Celts living in Galatia at this time. Ask: How do the characteristics unique to your culture help you to hear and receive the gospel message? Which of these characteristics makes you susceptible to losing your new identity in Christ because of interference from other believers? Next, invite participants to consider their families of origin and the communities and cultures in which they were reared. Ask: Which characteristics of how you were reared helped you to be receptive to and embrace the gospel? Which ones make you susceptible to losing your identity as a follower of Christ?

The "Beginnings" section states, "Paul was content that Jewish Christians like him could remain ethnically Jewish. But he also felt that members of the larger Greco-Roman world should remain Greco-Roman and the Celtic believers should remain Celts while all proclaimed Christ" (page 11). Ask participants: What must remain from your old life when you start following Jesus?

What must not remain from your old life? How do you make sure that it does not?

**How It Works**

This section tells about Paul's circumstances and his relationship with the Galatians, including some of the stresses in that relationship. How does knowing the challenges the biblical writer faced help you to understand the Book of Galatians better? What help does that give you when dealing with stressful issues in your own life?

**Biblical Sanitizer**

The writer of the study introduces the concept of "clean and unclean." Through using examples about food eaten in different cultures, he helps us to understand that the concept is not referring to laundry or hand washing but to cultural differences and even prejudices. What is the difference between a viewpoint and a prejudice? When have you recognized that some attitude of yours was, in fact, a prejudice? In what ways does Christ call you to move beyond your prejudices?

Referring to the first century, the writer of the study says that "Christians broke all the rules by eating at a common table" (page 15). How do you do that today? Where do you need to do a better job of making room at your "table" for others?

The writer of the study also says, "We bless each other with the gift of acceptance" (page 15). What conditions, if any, should be on that acceptance? Do conditions make our openness to other Christians something less than acceptance?

Where does your faith in Jesus Christ move from believing to believing *and* doing?

## Live the Story

With the existence of so many Christian denominations, we often think that matters of doctrine or belief are what separate us. In reality, however, we actually hold faith in Christ in common; and the barriers are more often cultural. That is often true even about some of the places in our communities that might seem like mini-mission fields—that is, the folks there often believe in God and Christ even if they don't live their beliefs.

In what ways does this study of Galatians help you to see those cultural barriers as crossable? Which one(s) might your reading of Galatians suggest you should reach across? When and how might you do that?

## 2. Free to Be One in Christ

*Galatians 5:13–6:18*

### Faith Focus

As God's people, we live by the Spirit; and we fulfill God's law by loving our neighbor as ourselves.

### Before the Session

Read the chapter in the study and the assigned passage from Galatians.

The word *diversity* figures importantly in the "Claim Your Story" section and also serves as background to the whole chapter in the study. But it is not a neutral word in our society today; and for some participants, it may even have connotations of political correctness carried too far. Nonetheless, diversity is an important reality in society in general and in vital Christianity in particular. Give some thought to your own feelings about the word *diversity* so that if necessary, you can spur discussion of the word by sharing your own thoughts.

Have large sheets of paper or a markerboard and markers available for use in the "Claim Your Story" section.

### Claim Your Story

Write "diversity" on a markerboard or large sheet of paper. Invite group members to tell what definitions of that word come to mind. Jot those down on the markerboard or large sheet of paper as participants say them. When everyone who wants to contribute has done so, ask the group to consider the definitions and tell what feelings they have about them. If some of the definitions are negative, allow the contributors to air their feelings.

Then tell the group that while we may know of excesses in the name of diversity, the meaning behind it is positive. Diversity was a reality in the early church, and it has been a reality in the church ever since. (If any of the offered definitions support that claim, be sure to point them out.)

Next, ask participants to respond to the questions supplied by the writer in the "Claim Your Story" section of the study.

## Enter the Bible Story

### Read the Instructions

The missionaries from Jerusalem insisted that the Galatian Christians had to live under the whole law of the Old Testament. In contrast, Paul taught that they fulfilled the law by loving their neighbor. Part of the struggle for the Galatians was to decide who was right. The writer of the study helps us understand this concept by suggesting that rather than thinking of the Bible as an "instruction manual" for Christians, a better image is to think of it as a "map" that guides us on our journey but does not require us to put our ethnic identity aside to follow Jesus.

Read the last paragraph of the "Read the Instructions" section to your group. Then have the participants discuss the ways in which love and power are very different things.

### Then and Now

Paul's insistence that loving our neighbor as we love ourselves fulfilled the divine law (Galatians 5:14) means that Christians have an extraordinary amount of freedom to decide how to express that love. Freedom, however, can be misused. Refer participants to the Mickey Mantle example in the chapter in the study. Then ask them to read Galatians 5:13 and discuss what the verse means.

Next, ask participants to consider Galatians 5:15. Why would a discussion of Christian freedom lead to such a comment?

### So How Come?

While becoming Christians did not require the Galatian Celts to stop being Celts and try instead to become like the Jewish Christians, they nonetheless needed to cultivate the fruit of the Spirit. That meant that certain Celtic practices, such as sorcery and aggressive fighting, needed to be abandoned.

Ask your group to read Paul's list of the fruit of the Spirit and his related comments in Galatians 5:22-26. Why do you think he chose these particular characteristics as being from the Spirit of God?

Read to your group the paragraph in the "So How Come?" section of the study that begins, "We may still come across something wild and unplanned." How do we recognize isolated sins? If they are not really indicative of who we are, why should they still be rooted out?

**Tying It All Together**

The writer of the study points out that Paul seems to be making contradictory statements in Galatians 6:2 and 6:5. Ask participants to read both verses. Then note this comment from the writer of the study: "This is a great example of how biblical wisdom asks us to evaluate our present situation. There are times when we have to bear each other's burdens, but there are also times when it's important for us to carry our own load. It just depends" (page 25). What does it depend on?

The writer of the study also points out that Paul wanted the Celts to worship Jesus in ways consistent with their culture. In what ways does your style of worship reflect your ethnic identity and your culture?

## Live the Story

As Christians, we are free to love our neighbor as ourselves. Ask your group to consider the questions posed by the writer of the study in the "Live the Story" section of the chapter.

Let the last question ("What will you do with your freedom in Christ?") lead into a closing prayer in which you ask God to help each person present discover his or her personal answer to that question.

## 3. One of the Above

*Ephesians 1–3*

### Faith Focus

Although what we know about God and what we do for God often get broken apart, the grace of God through Jesus Christ brings them back together.

### Before the Session

At the end of the session, participants will be invited to give their Christian testimony using the vocabulary of Ephesians 2:8-10 or their own words. Many people find it difficult to give their testimony. Help participants do this by giving your own testimony. Give some thought now to what you might say and how you'd like to say it. If you think it would be helpful, jot down some notes or even write out your testimony.

### Claim Your Story

The writer of the study tells of seeing an old car that had Bible verses all over it—mostly warnings. Ask participants when they have encountered something like that (example: gospel tracts left in public restrooms). What was the primary (if undeclared) message of such "vehicles"? What effect, if any, do you think that message had on those who saw it?

The "Claim Your Story" section of the study asks three pertinent questions. Invite your group to suggest personal answers to each one.

### Enter the Bible Story

#### Introducing the Letter to the Ephesians

The writer of the study acknowledges that some Bible readers have questioned whether Paul is actually the author of Ephesians because its writing style is somewhat different from other letters by Paul. But the writer of the study gives a personal example about writing poems in different styles for different occasions.

Tell your group about the impact of Paul's preaching in Ephesus, where converts burned their books of magic. What items, if any, did you have to get rid of when you decided to follow Jesus? What elements of our culture today are inconsistent with Christianity?

Paul, says the writer of the study, wrote this letter "to demonstrate that the peace of Christ would create peace between Jew and Gentile and all humanity" (page 31). In what places do you see modern equivalents of that peace played out in the Christian community?

**Real Peace**

Paul peppered his opening remarks to the Ephesians with important faith concepts. The writer of the study comments on the peace of Christ (1:2), chosen to be holy (1:4), God's design revealed (1:9), saved by grace (2:8-10), and predestination (1:10; but be sure to look at what the writer of the study says about predestination not being about individuals).

Divide the group into five small groups. Assign each group one of the faith concepts. Have each group work together for five minutes to come up with a definition of their assigned concept, using the applicable verses and considering the overall content of Ephesians 1:1–2:10.

Bring the participants back together and ask: In what ways are these faith concepts still vital to Christian life today?

**Spirit of the Age**

The writer of the study defines the spirit of the age as "demonic forces" (page 34). While he doesn't mean that literally, he does mean that in every age there are culturally accepted attitudes, dispositions, and ideas that are contrary to the uniting force of the gospel. What are the "demonic forces" of our age? How do they work against the uniting force of the gospel?

The study writer explains that when Paul says, "I kneel before the Father" (Ephesians 3:14), he is not talking about a prescribed posture for prayer but a drop-to-his-knees awe of the God who recognizes and extends the gospel invitation to "every ethnic group in heaven or on earth" (3:15). Where do you see the church at large struggling with insider-outsider issues today? Where do you see our church struggling with these issues? Where do you personally struggle with them?

This section of the study concludes with a mention of theological fads as opposed to true love among believers. What concepts seem to be theological fads today? How do you differentiate a fad from a practice or concept of ongoing worth?

**Live the Story**

The Christian experience is not "one size fits all." The questions posed by the writer in the "Live the Story" section of the study are useful for bringing the various threads of the session together. Ask the participants to consider and answer each question.

Finally, read again for the group Paul's words in Ephesians 2:8-10: "You are saved by God's grace because of your faith. This salvation is God's gift. It's not something you possessed. It's not something you did that you can be proud of. Instead, we are God's accomplishment." Ask group members what it means to be "God's accomplishment." In what ways can the vocabulary of these verses be formed into a personal testimony?

Let any participants who are willing give their testimony to the group, using the vocabulary of Ephesians 2:8-10 or any other language they prefer.

## 4. House Rules

*Ephesians 4–6*

### Faith Focus

The evidence of our reconciliation with God shows in the specifics of our daily lives.

### Before the Session

Read Chapter 4 in the study and Ephesians 4–6. At the end of the session, participants will be invited to share personal struggles in reconciling their lives with God's plan. Be prepared to tell a personal anecdote regarding changes you've had to make in this vein. What have you had to sacrifice to bring your way of life in line with God's desires?

Have pencils and note cards available for the participants.

### Claim Your Story

The writer of the study tells an anecdote from his time in seminary. Ask participants what point they take from it. Why do you think the writer used this as an example of a cosmic battle of good and evil?

Read the questions at the end of the "Claim Your Story" section in the study. Ask everyone to think about some personal examples. Then invite participants to share answers with the group. Share your personal examples to initiate the conversation.

What are you likelier to believe, what a person says or what a person does? Can you give an example where a person's actions were more important than his or her beliefs? If someone were to look at your life without knowing you personally, would it be evident from your actions that you are a follower of Christ?

## Enter the Bible Story

### The Household of God

Paul spoke of how Christians in the Ephesian households should interrelate and said those relationships should mirror the relationship between Christ and the church. Ephesians 5:22–6:9 refers to some issues that are uncomfortable for us today, such as the submissiveness of women and slavery. Read these verses together. What was Paul's aim in this passage? He wrote, "Submit to each other out of respect for Christ" (5:21). What are some societal rules under which you presently live that you may disagree with but still respect and submit to out of respect for God's wishes? How might you update Paul's advice for our time and culture?

The writer mentions the American civil rights movement. Since it could not directly regulate attitude, it instead worked to regulate behavior. How have America's racial attitudes nonetheless changed over time as a result of altered behavior? How have your racial attitudes changed?

Since early Christians couldn't change their government, they had to find harmonious ways to live as Christians under Roman rule. What are some things that you cannot presently change but about which you know you should nonetheless cultivate a more Christlike attitude?

### Communion Is Served

The Roman household was a complex and well-organized machine, typically including both familial and nonfamilial members. The writer of the study discusses the importance of women's roles both in running the household and in the church's worship. Did their prominence in these roles surprise you? Why, or why not?

What differences does the study writer point out between slavery in the time of the early church and slavery in American history?

The early Christian church operated principally out of private homes. What steps do you take to make your home accountable to God?

### Ready for Peace

Paul said the Christians in Ephesus were engaged in a cosmic battle between good and evil. Where are you called to do such cosmic battling today?

What was the principal distinction between Christ's peace and Rome's? Where do you see the peace of Christ in operation today?

Ask a volunteer to read to the group the excerpt from the letter to Diognetus quoted in the study. What do you find impressive in the letter? To what degree does it describe Christians today? To what degree does it describe you?

Just as Christians do now, the early Christians lived in an imperfect society with many things with which they might disagree. What are some modern struggles to maintain a godly household? What does this mean for you in terms of TV, the Internet, other influences, and cultural forces?

### Celebrate and Sing

Paul used marriage as an allegory for Christ and the church (Ephesians 5:32). What does that suggest about how we should view marriage or other relationships? What does marriage tell us about how we should relate with Christ?

Paul told the Ephesians that it was time to stop being spiritual infants (4:14). What does it mean to be a spiritual adult? What are some fads, Christian or otherwise, that tempt you these days? Are there prejudices you still hold that you know Christ wouldn't support? Beyond those the study writer mentions, what are some popular lies and distractions in our culture today?

## Live the Story

To the degree you can affect them, your environment and circumstances should reflect your relationship with Christ. How is that so in the environment of your household? Are there some changes you should make?

Hand out pencils and note cards. Ask participants to consider each of the questions in the "Live the Story" section of the study and then jot down their answers. Encourage those who are willing to talk about their particular struggles to do so. Ask these persons what small thing they each could change today in order to live in a way that is more in line with God's plan.

Conclude with a prayer, asking God to help each person to act on those changes.

# 5. Unquenchable Joy

*Philippians 1–2*

### Faith Focus

Joy—quite independent from circumstances—is the default setting of our lives when lived in Christ.

### Before the Session

Read Chapter 5 in the study and the first two chapters of Philippians. During your group discussion, participants will be asked to share some particular songs, movies, or other media—whether secular or religious—that have moved them. To get things started, be prepared to share one or two of your own experiences where your heart was touched by music or one of the arts.

## Claim Your Story

What point is the writer of the study making with his story about growing up in a military home? What really defines "home" for you? What larger identities give your life meaning?

Paul asked the Philippians to see themselves as citizens of heaven. Does that make sense for you today? If so, in what ways?

Read aloud the questions at the end of the "Claim Your Story" section in the study and invite participants to discuss them. What reasons can you offer for where you place God in terms of your allegiances?

## Enter the Bible Story

### A Prisoner for God

The writer of the study points out that even the worst situations in our lives can be used for the positive promotion of God's will in the world. Have bad circumstances in your own life ever served to advance Christ's work? If so, how did that make you feel?

Citizens of the Roman Empire felt pride at being Roman, even if they had never actually seen the capital. They were, at least, associated with Rome. What associations help define you? If other people were to try to define you by association, what might be their conclusions?

Paul's first convert in Philippi was a woman. How do women's roles in the early church seem similar to and/or different from those typical today?

Read the second-to-last paragraph in the "A Prisoner for God" section of the study (It begins, "The Philippian church was indeed..."). Is being "eclectic" a value in today's church? Why, or why not?

**The Commonwealth of Christ**

Paul's joy in the face of death seems paradoxical. What was at the core of this joy?

What complaints did Paul have about some people in the church? How does Paul's prayer in Philippians 1:10 remain relevant to us today?

Paul used citizenship to discuss the concept of larger identities as well as the right actions of citizens with respect to human authority. What did Paul say is a Christian's proper relationship with the state? What are the benefits of citizenship in God's kingdom? What are the responsibilities?

Ask a volunteer to read aloud the last two paragraphs of this section in the study. Discuss the questions included there and also this one: What should remain unique and what should be shared within the "commonwealth" of the faith community?

**They're Playing Our Song**

The writer of the study delves into the Christ hymn, found in Philippians 2:5-11. Read this passage together. What is the central message of the hymn? Why do you think Paul chose to include it at this point in the letter?

What is the value of music in helping us find meaning in life? What is its value in helping us in our walk with Christ? Point the group to the POW story in the study. Then invite participants to share how certain songs, poems, movies, art, or other media—whether secular or religious—have moved them. (Depending on the age and interests of your group, you might also want to suggest they think about novels, video games, and web-based initiatives as well.) How have any of these moved you to make life changes? to make faith commitments?

From this section of the study, read to the group the paragraph that begins, "The Roman emperor was considered to be a god..." and the two paragraphs that follow it. How did the mythology surrounding the Roman emperor help the Philippians understand the message of the Christ hymn? What is so important about Christ reducing himself to the level of a slave? What is the value and message behind the humiliation and horror associated with the cross and other acts of subservience by Jesus?

How did commonwealth function in Paul's context? Additionally, what did Paul have to say about dying? How can slavery equal joy?

### Live the Story

Most Christians have chosen not to live together in a communal way. Why don't such communal arrangements usually work in the real world? What is the larger point we can take from Paul's words in Philippians 1:27?

The core of the joy articulated in Paul's letter comes from anticipating the resurrection. How can Christ's joy remain independent from one's physical circumstances in the meantime?

Read aloud the questions listed at the end of this section in the study. In particular, invite participants to share personal examples regarding the final question. What needs to change to make Christ's joy more present and evident in your everyday routine?

Conclude with prayer. You might want to thank God for the willing sacrifices of so many members of the early church, for the hope of resurrection, and for the reality of Christian joy.

## 6. The Heart of Joy

*Philippians 3–4*

### Faith Focus

Our life in Christ is a journey toward the goal of resurrection from the dead.

### Before the Session

Read Philippians 3–4 and Chapter 6 in the study. In the opening section, the study writer points out how often conflicts within congregations are over trivial concerns. He's not calling for an "ain't it awful" session, where we wallow in examples of bad behavior among church members. Rather, the study writer is simply setting the stage for us to understand one of the challenges the Philippian church faced.

Therefore, while you might want to have participants mention one or two church member fights just to identify with this issue, it's important that you soon steer the session toward Paul's positive advice about working for the good of the commonwealth, being glad in the Lord, and recognizing our life in Christ as a journey toward the goal of resurrection.

### Claim Your Story

Read the "Claim Your Story" section of the study to the group. Then invite participants to consider briefly the questions included. Especially urge participants to share stories of church member conflicts where other church members were able to help the opponents achieve a peaceful resolution.

How have you let yourself be distracted from what's most important in church life? How did you find your way back?

### Enter the Bible Story

### The Finish Line

The study writer tells about completing a marathon despite having lost all motivators except his sense of duty. Invite participants to tell their personal stories of competitive sports or working for a "personal best." Ask what sacrifices they made to achieve their goal.

Ask a volunteer to read aloud Philippians 3:10-14, where Paul uses the language of athletic training. What is Paul's reason for doing so? What is his point about endurance? What did Paul focus on that kept him running?

In what ways do athletic endeavors serve as compelling allegories for our life with Christ?

Consider the quality of endurance in your own life of faith and the first passage quoted from John Chrysostom in the study (page 61). What are Christians "training" for? What are common distractions? Who are the "enemies of the cross" Paul refers to in Philippians 3:18-19?

The study writer discusses statistics that rank winners and losers. What do you keep statistics about? What are the statistics that really matter in the life of faith?

Ask a volunteer to read aloud Philippians 4:8-9. In what sense could those verses apply to the idea of religious statistics?

**Not Worth Spit**

Paul addressed two distractions threatening the church in Philippi. This section discusses the first: Jewish Christians who insisted that the Gentile believers in Philippi adopt Jewish practices.

When have you seen someone urge a congregation to adopt the practices or attitudes of a church with which that person was formerly associated? What was the outcome? What parts of worship practice are based in local custom or tradition? What parts are universal to the church?

What is the point of the study writer's anecdote regarding Los Angeles versus Indiana (pages 61–62)? How do differing cultural qualities distract us from Christ's message? What can we do to avoid this pitfall? What could you do this week to open yourself to an unfamiliar cultural practice that might help you better understand other Christians?

What was happening in Philippi to which Paul felt he needed to respond with his "stats" (Philippians 3:4-6)? What clout or "street cred" does Paul's preconversion history give his message? Why did Paul think so little of his own stats (3:7)? Isn't it a good thing to follow the law?

What objective did Paul articulate as truly worth our focus and endurance (Philippians 3:10-11)?

**One Step After Another**

In this section of the study, the writer focuses on the second problem in the Philippian church: Two church members—Euodia and Syntyche (4:2)—were at odds with each other. Their conflict was apparently spilling over into the congregation. The study writer says, "A good grudge in the name of Christ can go on for years" (page 63). Why is that so? Why does the study writer say a church grudge is like the Olympic Games? How should they be different?

The study writer points out that Paul's letter, calling for Euodia and Syntyche to reconcile and for the congregation to help that reconciliation, would have been read aloud in the congregation, with Euodia and Syntyche present. How would some form of that technique help today when church members are squabbling? What is the larger point about the commonwealth of Christ? What is our individual responsibility as a part of this commonwealth?

Why do you think Paul moved directly from urging reconciliation to calling for gladness in the Lord (Philippians 4:4)? What can we learn from the way Paul buffered his critical remarks with joy and praise?

What does the study writer say was an upside of Paul's imprisonment? The study writer closes this section with a second quotation from John Chrysostom (pages 65–66). How does this passage help to summarize Paul's message?

**Live the Story**

Read the "Live the Story" section in the study to the class. Discuss the questions included.

End with a prayer requesting a greater ability to base our actions on Christ's hope and joy.